How to
Survive
Getting Your
Kid into College

WARNING:

This guide contains differing opinions. Hundreds of heads will not always agree. Advice taken in combination may cause unwanted side effects. Use your head when selecting advice.

How to Survive

Getting Your
Kid into College

by Hundreds of Happy Parents Who Did

RACHEL KORN, SPECIAL EDITOR

Hundreds of Heads Books, LLC

ATLANTA

Cover photograph by Michael Kemter (man/son), Rubberball Productions (center
woman/daughter), Blend Images, LLC (right woman/daughter)

Cover and book design by Elizabeth Johnsboen

Library of Congress Cataloging-in-Publication Data

How to survive getting your kid into college / Rachel Korn, special editor.
   p. cm.
ISBN-13: 978-1-933512-11-2
1. Universities and colleges--United States--Admission. 2. College choice--United States.
I. Korn, Rachel.
LB2343.32.H677 2007
378.1'610973--dc22

2007015723

See page 227 for credits and permissions.

HUNDREDS OF HEADS™ books are available at special discounts when purchased in bulk
for premiums or institutional or educational use. Excerpts and custom editions can be created for specific uses. For more information, please email sales@hundredsofheads.com or
write to:

HUNDREDS OF HEADS BOOKS, LLC
#230
2221 Peachtree Road, Suite D
Atlanta, Georgia 30309

ISBN-10: 1-933512-11-3
ISBN-13: 978-1933512-11-2

Printed in U.S.A.
10 9 8 7 6 5 4 3 2 1

CONTENTS

Logic dictates that the college admissions process is stressful on the applicants, but too often, parental stress is overlooked. When I was an admissions officer speaking to parents, I often saw fear, panic, and pleas for help in their eyes: "Tell me what I can do to help my child get in!" You may not expect to feel all the same emotions as your child, but the admissions hysteria is contagious.

With all the uncertainty and variables in the college admissions process, more and more parents are feeling that they have less and less control. You don't know what you don't know about the admissions process, and you have to rely on your high school, the admissions officers, your peers, and books to guide you and your child to perfection—his dream school.

What about that fear that you are not doing things "right," which will drive you crazy through this journey with your child? Take heart: you are not alone, and it is essentially impossible to do everything "right."

Stay strong. You have weapons and armor in this battle for your sanity— the power to take control of the fear and trust that everything will eventually work out.

I know this isn't easy. But the experiences and lessons learned from hundreds of other parents who have "been there, done that," will help. Along with a solid analysis of the college application journey as it applies to parents, that's what you'll find in this book.

Laugh with and learn from the advice presented here, and you will survive.

—RACHEL KORN

THE HEADS EXPLAINED

With hundreds of tips, stories, and advice in this book, how can you quickly find those golden nuggets of wisdom? Of course, we recommend reading the entire book, but you can also look for these special symbols:

 Remember this significant story or advice.

 This may be something to explore in more detail.

 Watch out! Be careful! (Can we make it any clearer?)

 We are astounded, thrilled, or delighted by this one.

Here's something to think about.

Number of kids in college.

—THE EDITOR
AND HUNDREDS OF HEADS BOOKS

CHAPTER 1

Sizing Things Up: When to Start & What to Do

There are few life events as redefining for a family as a child's college admission. In one fell swoop, you are making heavy decisions about your child's future through a process that challenges your values, your mental health, and your skills as a parent. You have probably been thinking about your child's college education since the day he was born. The pressure only grows when you read all the media coverage about the difficulties of college admissions. Every fall and spring—the time of applications and of answers—you are inundated with information about this scary process.

According to some "experts," you should be shaping your child's experience from the beginning of high school and packaging him into an expert in one or several areas. You should be touring colleges and hiring tutors to prevent any possible flaw. Is this realistic? Maybe. Is it healthy? No way. So when should you start the admissions process?

While every child has his own "start date," there are things you can do early on, such as planning overall high school coursework and helping him find activities he loves. Testing and college touring can wait until junior year. It's hard to find the balance between pushing your child to maximize his high school career and letting your kid be a kid. Very few families these days achieve this balance, much to everyone's chagrin (and yes, to the chagrin of admissions officers). Take it slow. Encourage your children to study and engage in activities, and not start the rat race until the PSAT or PACT in 10th grade.

What role will you have in this process—dictator, supervisor, partner, or absentee? Lay the groundwork during the beginning and planning phases of the process to establish the relationship you will have with your child. Try to start off on the right foot—supportive, helpful, but trusting. Giving your child guidance and freedom to explore will empower him, and by the time he reaches college, he will have the confidence in himself to succeed—checking in with you along the way, of course.

I WOULDN'T WAIT UNTIL SENIOR YEAR to start the application process. By fall semester, my son had driver's education, three AP classes, a bunch of Boy Scout events, and college research and applications. He was overwhelmed.

—RICHARD TYLER
REDMOND, WASHINGTON
🎓 1
🏛 NEW MEXICO INSTITUTE OF MINING & TECHNOLOGY

• • • • • • • •

THE BEST TIME FOR YOUR CHILD to start thinking about college is during middle school, because college is an aspiration and you have to cultivate a mentality to go to college. Students have to want to know how to do things and you have to inform them that their skills are going to support them for the rest of their lives. The earlier you do that, the easier it is for your child to get into the college-prep mode.

—GLYNIS RAMOS-MITCHELL
ATLANTA, GEORGIA
🎓 2
🏛 MIDDLEBURY COLLEGE; UNIVERSITY OF MASSACHUSETTS, AMHERST

• • • • • • • •

WE STARTED TOURING COLLEGES during our daughter's sophomore year in high school; looking back now, I think it was too soon. What my daughter liked and disliked in schools in tenth grade actually changed by the time she was a senior. They change so much in those three years.

—T.S.
LOS ANGELES, CALIFORNIA
🎓 1
🏛 DUKE UNIVERSITY

I STARTED THINKING ABOUT APPLYING to college when my daughter started high school. I went to all of the PTA meetings and I went to college fairs. I'm an artist and I don't think so much with my left brain, I'm not that methodical and I don't navigate the world like other people. It was really important to me to be informed in order to make sure that I didn't blow it. I worried I would let a deadline slip or miss something, so I was on top of all of it at every moment.

—ANONYMOUS
LOS ANGELES, CALIFORNIA
🍷 1
🏛 UNIVERSITY OF CALIFORNIA, SANTA BARBARA

· · · · · · · · ·

No school makes you happy or smart. You have to do that on your own, so relax about making the choice of schools the "right decision" and focus on making the decision of school "right."

—BETH REINGOLD GLUCK
ATLANTA, GEORGIA
🍷 1

BETTER LATE THAN NEVER

Don't force your kids to start looking at colleges if they aren't ready. I bought a college guide and moved it around the house every so often, but my son didn't get around to reading it until the summer after his junior year. I had friends who had kids who were motivated during their freshman years, so I thought maybe there was something wrong with mine. But then I went to a college-admissions Web site and found other parents who were also tearing out their hair over their late bloomers. It was very reassuring to find so many other parents who couldn't get their kids motivated. It's like toilet training; you can go on about it for years, but they aren't going to learn it until they are ready.

—C.K.
Larkspur, California
1
Whitman College

YOU CAN'T REALLY RELY ON YOUR KID'S SCHOOL guidance counselor to know all the information you will need. Go to those after-school nights where they discuss financing, testing and other issues. And you should start going when your child is in the 10th grade; don't wait until their senior year. Some would say 9th grade!

—SHERRY APPEL
WASHINGTON, D.C.
2
JOHNSON & WALES UNIVERSITY

. . . .

WE DIDN'T START DOING ANYTHING until we got his first batch of test scores to give us some kind of idea of what level we should be looking at. He's a really bright kid so we had some idea. And as much as we hate standardized tests, it gave us some place to start.

—ANONYMOUS
BROOKLYN, NEW YORK
1
BROWN UNIVERSITY

. . . .

START PREPARING FOR COLLEGE in your child's junior year— maybe even the end of sophomore year. That is the perfect time for your child to look at various colleges and become aware of different types of college settings.

—M.H.
ELLENWOOD, GEORGIA
1
LANDER UNIVERSITY

ADMISSIONS ARITHMETIC

Why all the hysteria about college admissions? Take a look at today's college math:

Population bubble of high school students
+   the Common Application (easier to apply)
+   more applications to more schools
+   pressure to improve college's rankings
+   static university class size
───
=   increasing difficulty gaining admission to top universities.

Today's high school students face this "perfect storm" of admissions factors, and the conversion of all these factors in the admissions process increases the competition at the "hot" schools. Quite simply, college admission is all about supply and demand. Right now, there is limited supply and great demand. Schools have the luxury of being even more selective, and the average, good student is struggling more than ever to stand out.

But there is good news: there are thousands of colleges and universities in the U.S. and Canada. Although it feels like a race for the prestigious, "name" schools, those are not always the best places for your children. There are marvelous educational opportunities everywhere. Yes, admission is harder than ever right now, but with thorough research, a positive attitude about the college search, and thoughtful applications, your child will succeed.

DON'T LET THE RUMOR MILL GRIND YOU DOWN

One of the biggest frustrations college admissions officers face are the rumor mills that crank out stories about their universities and their admissions policies that are not based on fact but nevertheless are circulated as gospel: X University hates students from a certain high school; X University only accepts students with high test scores; X University wants only athletes and student-government presidents.

The most dangerous elements in this rumor mill are Web sites and blogs where people share their experiences and supposed "insider knowledge" about admissions. The truth is, no one knows how applications are evaluated except admissions officers, and no person who has simply been through the process knows how admissions officers think. The advice on these Web sites can really lead you and your child astray. Make sure to separate fact from fiction by taking anything not relayed by official college admissions materials or by college professionals with a shaker of salt.

I STARTED AN EXCEL SPREADSHEET for each of my kids when they were freshmen in high school, and it was really helpful when applying to colleges and for scholarships. List all awards (academic, athletic, everything), community service, jobs, and anything else relevant. Make sure to include dates, contacts, hours volunteered, and any other specific information. That way, when you or your student starts to fill out all those wonderful forms, you will have all the information at your fingertips, in chronological order. I found it to be invaluable.

—SANDY
LOVELAND, OHIO
🎓 2
🏛 OHIO STATE UNIVERSITY

• • • • • • • •

I HIRED A PRIVATE COUNSELOR who could help my son find a school that would suit him. We hired her during the fall semester of his senior year in college, which was a little too late. It all worked out, but I would tell other parents to start earlier. The counselor got him involved in the process, which is what I was really unsuccessful at. So if you have unmotivated children, hire someone, but do it during their junior year.

—MARYANNE LAGUARDIA
SANTA MONICA, CALIFORNIA
🎓 2
🏛 BELOIT COLLEGE; UNIVERSITY OF ARIZONA

There's a school for everybody. Enjoy the process. Don't get yourself frantic. And if the decision is wrong, it can be changed.

— MARLA
BOCA RATON,
FLORIDA
🏛 UNIVERSITY
OF FLORIDA;
FLORIDA STATE
UNIVERSITY

NEVER TOO EARLY, PART 1

When your children are around eight years old, get a job with a university that has tuition benefits! Those benefits generally kick in after seven or eight years of employment, and often cover not only tuition for the school you work for but also that of many other universities. Through domestic partner benefits, Washington University in St. Louis is footing the entire bill for my children's tuition at two different colleges—and neither one of them even goes to Washington U.

—N.L.
St. Louis, Missouri
2
Truman State University;
California State University, Monterey Bay

DISCUSSION ABOUT THE COLLEGE application process should begin during your kids' sophomore year. In their junior years help your kids start making a list of colleges they would like to attend and analyzing various aspects of those college's applications. By the time they're seniors, they'll have experience with the application process and how everything works.

—R.F.
LITHONIA, GEORGIA
🎓 3
🏫 DUKE UNIVERSITY; UNIVERSITY OF MIAMI (2)

• • • • • • • •

MY DAUGHTER AND I STARTED PREPARING for college her junior year. Her plan was that when she started her senior year, she would know what college she would be attending. She had her heart set on Southern Illinois University in Carbondale. She applied, got in, got her housing plan together, and by October of her senior year, she was good to go. All I did was brag to my friends about how my daughter was going to college.

—AUDREY DAVIS
CHICAGO, ILLINOIS
🎓 2
🏫 SOUTHERN ILLINOIS UNIVERSITY; ROBERT MORRIS COLLEGE

A LOT OF PARENTS TAKE THEIR KIDS to tour different campuses after they get accepted, but I think it's better to go on tours even before you apply. First of all, the application process is really cumbersome; you can't use the same essay for every school, so why not eliminate some work? The application fees are expensive, so why not narrow down your choices early on? And also, once you get accepted, you have such a short time to make a decision; you probably wouldn't have time to see everything. For us it worked out great.

—J.H.
PASADENA, CALIFORNIA
2
UNIVERSITY OF SOUTHERN CALIFORNIA

· · · · · · · ·

I don't think starting a year in advance is too much. You have a lot of stuff to do. Don't let your kids procrastinate. You can't do this the right way if you're rushing.

— MARLA
BOCA RATON, FLORIDA
2
UNIVERSITY OF FLORIDA; FLORIDA STATE UNIVERSITY

NO GUARANTEES, NO REGRETS

There are "experts" in the Web world who advise parents that the way to guarantee admission to a top college is to plan a child's whole life—whether he likes it or not—beginning way before high school. It horrifies admissions officers that families believe they must resort to such tactics.

Adopting this philosophy exacts a high cost. Do you really want him or her to plug away at a set of fake activities, lose four years of high school's developmental experiences, and, perhaps, still not get into that dream school?

Rejecting this philosophy means you're thumbing your nose at scare tactics. Know and remember that there are no guarantees in selective admission, ever; no matter what your child's profile. If you can make peace with this idea, you will succeed in every part of this process: conquering the fear that will in turn make your child stressed; balancing hopes and dreams with reality; and managing the April admissions notifications healthfully.

THE FIRST THING WE DID was go to a college fair the summer after sophomore year of high school. My son fell in love with California Institute of Technology at the fair and that is where he ended up going. You can probably find out about these fairs through your kid's high school. I think it was a good introduction for us to many of the options out there.

> —JILLIAN
> OAKLAND, CALIFORNIA
> 🎓 1
> 🏛 CALIFORNIA INSTITUTE OF TECHNOLOGY

• • • • • • • • •

TRY TO CONVINCE YOUR KIDS to get a little bit out of their comfort zone when they are looking at potential schools to go to. As a ranch kid from Texas, where our closest neighbor is two miles away, my daughter only wanted to go to a very small and rural school. So I let her pick the colleges she wanted to visit and when we planned our trip there I would say, "Since we're headed to Kentucky, let's just stop in Memphis on the way and take a look at some schools." We ended up checking out 40 schools this way, and she ended up at that school in Memphis, where she never would have thought about going had I not convinced her to expand her horizons.

> —TOM
> WACO, TEXAS
> 🎓 1
> 🏛 RHODES COLLEGE

MY SON KNEW HE WANTED to be a journalist as a freshman in high school and he also knew where he wanted to go to college. Since he was totally certain, all we could do was help him to create and improve his résumé. He wrote a newsletter for his high school, interned at a small community paper and went to writing workshops around the country. He ultimately got in, mainly because he had exactly the background that the school was looking for.

—BERNIE
HOUSTON, TEXAS
1
NORTHWESTERN UNIVERSITY

• • • • • • • • •

ENCOURAGE YOUR CHILD TO PICK two or three extracurricular activities that he or she really cares about. My son was heavily involved with a youth robotics competition, and he was always asked about it. His other major activities were Scouts and a varsity letter in track. Every admissions officer told us that a strong record of commitment to a few things is a lot better than a scattershot listing of dozens of things.

—RICHARD TYLER
REDMOND, WASHINGTON
1
NEW MEXICO INSTITUTE OF MINING & TECHNOLOGY

I gave my daughters good advice on the things they should do to get into college. I told them they should not be apathetic about anything.

—LAURA ROMANO
SAN DIEGO, CALIFORNIA
UNIVERSITY OF CALIFORNIA, SAN DIEGO; CLAREMONT MCKENNA COLLEGE

I STARTED WITH *COLLEGES THAT CHANGE LIVES,* which is a book that profiles 40 colleges that are great schools for late bloomers. I read most of the big statistical books about schools and relied on *The Princeton Review* and the College Board for information. My kids had B averages in high school so I was determined to pick schools that they would get into, as opposed to big reaches. A counselor once said to me that it is not where you can get in, it is where you can stay in, so I wanted to make sure that my kids wouldn't end up coming home after their first semesters.

—MARYANNE LAGUARDIA
SANTA MONICA, CALIFORNIA
🎓 2
🏛 BELOIT COLLEGE; UNIVERSITY OF ARIZONA

. . . .

It's not your job to choose for them, but you can help them become more aware of what is out there.

—TOM
WACO, TEXAS
🎓 1
🏛 RHODES COLLEGE

NEVER TOO EARLY, PART 2

I started attending college meetings at my son's high school when he was a freshman. The meetings were for parents of sophomores and juniors, and even though parents looked at me like I was crazy for starting so early, I am glad that I chose to go when I did. If I didn't attend these meetings when I did, I would have never known about the SAT II. Many of the schools my son applied to required the SAT II subject test and what I learned at the meeting was if you know ahead of time that your child needs to take it, then enroll him or her in the honors classes because those classes teach subject matter closest to what is on the test. I also learned to plan to take the tests right after completion of the class since the material is still fresh at that point. If I hadn't known all of this, my son might not have enrolled in honors chemistry, for example, and then he might not have had enough information to do well on the exam.

—ANONYMOUS
DEERFIELD, ILLINOIS
🎓 1
🏛 VANDERBILT UNIVERSITY

IF YOUR HIGH SCHOOL OFFERS an organized trip to visit college campuses, send your kids, even if they are planning visits to colleges your kids are not interested in. We convinced our daughter to go and it was totally worth it. She was able to compare large campuses and small campuses, urban versus rural, and high-rise versus small dorms. It's so important, given an opportunity like this. They can identify aspects of college that they don't even know exist.

—J.M.
ARLINGTON, VIRGINIA
🎓 2
🏛 LEHIGH UNIVERSITY; ELON UNIVERSITY

• • • • • • • •

IF YOU GET A LATE START LIKE I DID, state schools would be a good option because they usually have extended deadlines. My son was supposed to go into the army but he ended up getting a medical discharge. It was pretty late in the game and a lot of deadlines had already passed. As soon as he was discharged I immediately got on the Web and researched deadline dates. Since I had residency in Oregon, we determined that Oregon State was the best choice, and we also had enough time to make the deadline.

—STEPHEN
VANCOUVER, WASHINGTON
🎓 2
🏛 FURMAN UNIVERSITY; OREGON STATE UNIVERSITY

THERE ARE TWO GAMES YOU CAN PLAY in this college admissions process. One is for private schools; the other is for public. At a public state school the admissions board looks at the numbers; they don't take into account the types of classes you took. Therefore, your strategy would be for your kid to take the easier classes in order to guarantee A's. Private schools, on the other hand, do take into account the level of classes, so you would want to have your kids sign up for the more challenging high school courses.

—ANONYMOUS
DEERFIELD, ILLINOIS
1
VANDERBILT UNIVERSITY

• • • • • • • • •

PARENTS MUST BE REALISTIC. First, anything you recall about college is at least a quarter century out of date. Second, if you can, rely on Web-based tools that show recent acceptance statistics (even results for applicants from your own high school) based on GPA and SAT/ACT results. Use the data to find realistic target schools—no point in urging the student to try for the Ivy League if your kid's stats aren't even on the same page.

—TOM
SAN FRANCISCO, CALIFORNIA
1
UNIVERSITY OF ARIZONA

NEVER TOO EARLY, PART 3

START ADDING COLLEGE TOURS to your family vacations. Do it in conjunction with other attractions you are going to see. Make it a happy family bonding experience with no pressure. When my son was in eighth grade we traveled to the East Coast for a month-long vacation. While we were there we stopped by several schools. When the time came for my son to apply he had a clue as to what that part of the country was like.

—ANONYMOUS
PORTLAND, OREGON
1
STANFORD UNIVERSITY

· · · · · · · · ·

FIND SOME KIND OF BACK-DOOR ENTRANCE to introduce your kids to college campuses. You want to start early, but if you push too much before your kids are ready, they will just run. We live in Atlanta, pretty close to Emory. Emory has an Egyptian museum, so I planned a trip there. We also planned a lot of our college tours in conjunction with our vacations. A lot of families go to school after school, by the time they get to the last one the kids are burned out. We would ski, then go look at a school, go to a park, then look at a school.

—J.M.
MARIETTA, GEORGIA
1
RICE UNIVERSITY

IF YOU HAVE THE MONEY AND THE TIME, sign up for a study program at your first-choice school. My daughter attended a summer program at Smith College. She interviewed with an admissions officer while she was there, and was told that the college looks favorably at applicants who attended the program. She did get in, along with all the other girls who were in her class that summer.

—ANONYMOUS
PHILADELPHIA, PENNSYLVANIA
🎓 1
🏛 SMITH COLLEGE

• • • • • • • •

CASUALLY VISIT SOME LOCAL SCHOOLS that aren't of any interest before you even start the application process. We visited several schools in our town and nearby that our daughter knew she didn't want to attend, and it really helped her identify what she did and didn't want in a school. When she did get serious about applying, these background visits gave us a good foundation of knowledge and a good template with which to compare the schools she actually wanted to attend.

—LESLIE KUHLMAN
CINCINNATI, OHIO
🎓 1
🏛 FRANCISCAN UNIVERSITY OF STEUBENVILLE

START EARLY AND TAKE an informal approach. We took a campus tour with our son during a visit to his grandparents in his sophomore year of high school. We called a nearby school and scheduled a tour, just to let him get a feel for what a college visit is all about. There was no pressure because it was so early, and it helped him get an idea of what he wanted to look for in a school.

—DONNA
CINCINNATI, OHIO
2
MIAMI UNIVERSITY

. . . .

DON'T DISMISS THE OBSCURE liberal arts schools. My son found the perfect fit! Do your own research. Don't just look at the rankings. My son found a small liberal arts school called Whitman College, so I immediately went online to study the college's Web site. We went to visit the campus and I spoke to relatives and friends in the school's area. Everyone raved about the school. I can't imagine a better school for him. I really stayed away from the rankings because they are so influenced by politics, money and media. It creates this false idea that there is one size that fits all.

—C.K.
LARKSPUR, CALIFORNIA
1
WHITMAN COLLEGE

HOW SELECTIVE?

What does it mean when a college guide names a certain school "very selective"? Here's a yardstick:

Less selective: Applicants need to meet minimum requirements and demonstrate interest in college-level study. Test scores are used for course placement.

More selective: Grades, recommendations, course work and essays are considered along with test scores.

Very selective: There are as many as 10 or 15 applications for every spot. Fewer than 100 colleges in the country are considered to be in this category.

SPECIAL CONSIDERATIONS

There are schools out there for everyone. My oldest son was diagnosed with ADD as a senior in high school. We thought he would be more successful in a smaller classroom where attendance was required, and where he would be held accountable for his whereabouts. Because of this we encouraged him to go to a small private school. My second child had an interest in equine science, which wasn't offered at any state schools, and she also had an interest in photography as a major. The school she found was the only one that offered both of those majors. My third child also has ADD and he likes one-on-one interaction, he likes to talk to his teachers, and he likes discussions. It's hard to find this at a state school.

—ANONYMOUS
HICKORY, NORTH CAROLINA
♆ 3
⚒ ELON UNIVERSITY; VIRGINIA INTERMONT COLLEGE;
WAKE FOREST UNIVERSITY

KEEPING YOUR EXPECTATIONS AT BAY begins well before college, when you learn that living your life through your child is not always healthy. They have their own goals, which may not be your goals; you and your child will be happier if you can realize that. My daughter made very good decisions, so it's easy to be philosophical now. But parents whose egos are all wrapped up in where their kids go to college are depriving their children of the opportunity to grow and mature.

—R.F.
ATLANTA, GEORGIA
🎓 1
🏛 UNIVERSITY OF PENNSYLVANIA

· · · · · · · ·

THE PSAT SEEMS TO START THE CLOCK ticking and also provide the first idea of how high a student can realistically aspire. I do think the time-honored notion of a summer visit schedule at the end of the junior year provides a nice anchor that everyone can recognize in terms of narrowing focus. Too early and the student is likely to feel pressure and begin viewing the whole process as an interminable burden.

—EDWARD HERSHEY
PORTLAND, OREGON
🎓 3
🏛 CORNELL UNIVERSITY (2), COLORADO COLLEGE

IT IS REALLY IMPORTANT TO KNOW your child realistically. We all think our children are the best and brightest—some of them are—but for those who are not, if you don't open your eyes, you are seeing what you want your kids to be, not who they really are and what they are really capable of.

—MELISSA
LOS ANGELES, CALIFORNIA
🏆 1
🎓 UNIVERSITY OF CALIFORNIA, SAN DIEGO

• • • • • • • •

WE STARTED TALKING ABOUT COLLEGE with our son in his junior year, prompted by a note from his guidance counselor telling us about college night. Our son definitely wanted to go to college at that point, but I wanted to make sure it was his desire and not my desire for him to go. I left it alone until another college night; until he said again, "Let's go!"

—ROBIN MALKI
WEST ORANGE, NEW JERSEY
🏆 1
🎓 BLOOMSBURG UNIVERSITY

• • • • • • • •

Consider

MY SON ALWAYS KNEW what he wanted to study since he was in eighth grade. Because of this, I was advised to have him do things related to that field. He volunteered, he started his own organization, and he interned during the summers. He was able to show his true passion in his college application and support it with actual experience.

—G.V.
HOUSTON, TEXAS
🏆 2
🎓 UNIVERSITY OF TEXAS, AUSTIN; UNIVERSITY OF MICHIGAN

EVEN IF YOUR CHILD KNOWS he or she wants to major in science or computers, make sure he doesn't apply only to technology schools. My son wanted to get into computer science for years and thought he only needed to apply to schools like MIT and Caltech. I didn't think that was such a good idea, so I told him that I wanted him to look at some small liberal arts schools with good technology programs. When he went to visit the Rochester School of Technology on their exploration weekend he realized that a small liberal arts school might be better for him.

—KATHIE
COOPERSBURG, PENNSYLVANIA
🎓 2
🏫 PRINCIPIA COLLEGE; ROANOKE COLLEGE

* * * * * * * *

IF YOU THINK YOUR KIDS are making choices that aren't the best fit for them, think of a way to introduce the reality of their choices before they make a final decision. My older one thought she wanted to go to NYU, so I signed her up for a summer program at a college in a big city to see what a college campus in that environment was like. When she finished the summer, she realized that a city campus might not be for her. Even though I knew NYU wasn't a good fit, I couldn't tell her not to go, or that she couldn't go. That's a surefire way to send your kids running.

—L.L.
GLOBAL NOMAD
🎓 2
🏫 HARVARD UNIVERSITY; BROWN UNIVERSITY

HELP YOUR KIDS BE REALISTIC about the application process. I encouraged my son to look at the schools' 25-75-percent profiles and to compare himself to these descriptions. I talked him out of applying to Duke, because his numbers were on the low end of their profile. But, when we looked at MIT, for example, we saw that with his strong science, math and tech background, he had a really good chance.

—JORDAN CASELL
STAFFORD, VIRGINIA
🖋 1

. . . .

THE BEST COLLEGE DOES NOT GUARANTEE a successful future. A big-name school is just another way for parents to brag. Encourage your children to do their best in high school and be passionate about something they believe in. Your children will succeed in any college they want to attend. All they need today is a diploma, a love of life, and a passion for their career.

—DEE A. MARTIN
MADEIRA, OHIO
🖋 4
🏛 UNIVERSITY OF DAYTON; WITTENBERG UNIVERSITY;
BOSTON UNIVERSITY; SAINT LOUIS UNIVERSITY

YOUR CHILD'S SPECIAL TALENTS

College-application time is a major period of personal assessment for your child. He has to ask himself: Who am I? What do I love and value? What do I want to do with my life? These are philosophical, self-defining moments in his life. It is your moment to talk to him about his dreams and help him plan the path to achieving them; however, it is also the time to help him find something that will be achievable. It is sad to watch parents push their students to apply to schools where admissions chances are extremely low, or where the school and the student are not a good match. If you know your son is not going to be an Olympic athlete or the next Yo Yo Ma, then help him find a place where he does not have to be a superstar. If he has struggled with academics, point him toward schools where he can get extra support and where they will be happy to take him with his less-than-4.0 GPA. If your child is artistic, help him find a place to express his creativity. Your love, support and motivation for his dreams are critical to his self-esteem. The flip side of that coin is that it is also healthy parenting to guide your child to places where he will thrive instead of flounder. Of course, reach for the stars—just know your child and his needs.

WHAT ARE YOUR EXPECTATIONS?

Take time to investigate your own expectations, values, and biases about both the application process and your child's success. Are there certain schools you secretly—or not so secretly—wish he could attend? Is there a magic test score you want him to achieve? While you want the best for your child, you should be honest with yourself about what you really wish will happen. It is better to see, recognize, and process any selfish needs you may have so you can recognize it when your expectations are being unfairly put onto your child. As all parents do, you have hopes and dreams for him, but you will all be happier if you can be honest about whether your child shares them. Putting your expectations on him may, in fact, harm your child through unrealistic pressure. Your dream school, in fact, could be a mismatch. The car window decal that would make you proud could mean a miserable four years for your child. Set goals and share your dreams, but adjust your expectations to fit *his* dreams and ability.

NAVIANCE IS AN ONLINE PROGRAM that many school districts have. If you use it, you'll find information like: how many kids from your child's high school get accepted at certain campuses, and how many kids with comparable grades and scores to your child get accepted and rejected from campuses across the country. If your high school doesn't have this program, just go online to a college admissions Web site.

—R.K.
PHILADELPHIA, PENNSYLVANIA
🎓 1
🏛 UNIVERSITY OF PENNSYLVANIA

• • • • • • • • •

SO MANY PARENTS THINK ADMISSIONS officers are looking for well-rounded kids. While it is important that your children be exposed to many different things, I think it is better to find one passion. Find something they care deeply about. My daughter is a dancer and when she dances she comes alive, and when she writes about dancing, you know she loves it. That is what colleges want to hear.

—JOYCE
SCOTTSDALE, ARIZONA
🎓 1
🏛 UNIVERSITY OF MICHIGAN

MY YOUNGEST SON WAS DETERMINED; he wanted to do it all by himself. He liked talking to his friends and getting input from them. If he wanted my help, I would have been happy to assist him. I think it meant more to him because it was a big task that he took on himself and he enjoyed the challenge. He would run things by me to make sure I was in agreement with him; but other than that, he took care of it and I was proud of him.

—DEE DEE MELMET
REDWOOD CITY, CALIFORNIA
🏆 1
🏛 NORTHERN ARIZONA UNIVERSITY

THE ECHO BOOM

The children of baby boomers are working their way through the school system, and that's one of the reasons college applicants are so numerous. 3.2 million students graduated from high school in 2007; 3.1 million graduated in 2006. Compare these numbers with the 1993 statistic of 2.3 million graduates. The number of high school graduates is expected to reach its zenith in 2008, but applications will still outpace openings through 2010.

Money! College Costs & Your (Shrinking) Wallet

Almost as scary as the admissions process itself is the prospect of paying for this education. Even if money is no object, these four years are going to put a dent in your wallet and in your lifestyle. You will want to prepare yourself for this reality—your financial investment in your child—and be honest with yourself about how far you are truly willing to go. This is a real moment of truth for you. Consider the true limits of your financial capabilities to get a sense of the financial planning you need to do. Again, always remember that with aid and/or scholarship money, a private school can be as affordable as a public school.

The awful truth: your child may ultimately be admitted to his dream school—and yours—but without the right financial aid or financial planning, he will not be able to attend. It is best to be upfront about your finances. Transparency with your child about this part of the process will be crucial if his dream school is also a financial reach for the family. You will likely help him fill out all the financial aid forms and this will seem like "your" domain—but make this a family discussion, and be sure to set reasonable expectations.

The Internet has made the search for scholarships much easier, but applying still takes time and advance planning. Gaining a merit scholarship may be just as much of a reach as a reach school. Assess the reality of obtaining these scholarships; don't depend on getting one. You may need to apply quite early for scholarships, so take care not to miss deadlines. Financial aid, in other words is about planning, planning, planning.

I SPENT ABOUT $300 FOR COLLEGE TOURS, $100 for two ACT tests, $60 for an ACT prep class, $200 for college application fees, $5 on stamps for college applications, about $60 dollars in ink to print out draft after draft of college entrance essays, $20 in bus fare to attend college open houses, $150 on long-distance calls to colleges to ask about 30 minutes worth of questions every other day, $100 worth of transcripts, and about $500 on clothes and entertainment to console her when she didn't get into her first-choice school.

> —KEVIN ITSON
> CHICAGO, ILLINOIS
> 1
> UNIVERSITY OF ILLINOIS, URBANA-CHAMPAIGN

There are so many schol-arships out there; you just need to do a lot of research to find them.

—KAREN BARCHAS
TRUCKEE, CALIFORNIA
UNIVERSITY OF CALIFORNIA, BERKELEY

• • • • • • • • •

WE WANTED OUR DAUGHTER to apply for as many scholar-ships as possible so my husband thought up a little "incentive." We told her we'd give her 10 percent in cash of whatever scholarships she earned. If she got a $300 award, we gave her $30. Then she felt like there was something in it for her. She was eventually successful getting over $4,000 in scholarships!

> —TERESA OEFINGER
> PETALUMA, CALIFORNIA
> 1
> UNIVERSITY OF CALIFORNIA, DAVIS

WE CAN AFFORD QUITE A BIT, but I think $43,000-$45,000 per year is exorbitant when there are good alternatives that cost quite a bit less. My daughter really likes Boston, so her first thought was Boston College. She could probably get admitted there, but there would be no likelihood of financial aid. Same with some other small schools in the Northeast (Middlebury, Williams). So we looked at some more realistic alternatives in the Northeast and Northwest. These included Providence, University of Portland, Willamette University, and Illinois Wesleyan (which is my alma mater). These schools all have a very good overall student profile and very good reputations as schools that would provide an excellent education.

—ANONYMOUS
HIGHLANDS RANCH, COLORADO
📖 1

• • • • • • • •

DON'T OPEN SAVINGS ACCOUNTS in the children's names. Your child's assets are taken into account when determining their eligibility for financial aid. It is really tricky because I think most parents set up accounts in their children's names for the tax benefit. We started saving in our kids' names, but we got this information in time to correct it. We stopped putting money in their accounts and paid for college out of our own savings.

—ANONYMOUS
LOS ANGELES, CALIFORNIA
📖 2
🏫 CALIFORNIA STATE UNIVERSITY, NORTHRIDGE;
SANTA MONICA CITY COLLEGE

SCHOOL AID

One way I shrank college costs: I had a trunk party for my daughter. I invited family and friends to give her gifts before she left. I didn't really have to buy her anything. She received bedding, toiletries, school supplies, and money. I even had her call businesses to see if they had anything for college students that they would like to donate. She was given dry-erase boards, a hamper, artwork, socks, typing paper, calendars, and even detergent. This helped me financially and also helped her develop persuasive skills that will come in handy after college.

—MONICA FRAZIER
CHICAGO, ILLINOIS
🎓 1
🏛 GRAND VALLEY STATE UNIVERSITY

I HATE THE GOVERNMENT FORMS and invasiveness of financial aid and scholarships. We're paying cash. University of Arizona is a great deal on price; my daughter's old high school cost more.

—TOM
SAN FRANCISCO, CALIFORNIA
🎓 1
🏛 UNIVERSITY OF ARIZONA

I WAS SO PROUD THAT MY ONLY DAUGHTER was going to college. I was bragging to all my friends and family about her acceptance until I saw the annual tuition cost and her financial aid package. She had received a couple of grants, but 70 percent of her college education was loans. Since I didn't want my daughter to have to come out of college with over $30,000 in debt, I took the Parent Plus loan option. However, I didn't want that much in loans myself. So I called the financial aid office about three times a week to see what could be done to lower my loans. The financial aid office was so tired of me, they found four scholarships for my daughter. Her bill was only $3,000 when she graduated.

—DEBRA
CHICAGO, ILLINOIS
🎓 1
🏫 SOUTHERN ILLINOIS UNIVERSITY; WESTERN ILLINOIS UNIVERSITY

• • • • • • • • •

I HAVE SIX KIDS and have been going through a lengthy divorce. I had to sit down and tell my kids that they were going to have to get scholarships or take out loans for college because I couldn't afford to pay for it. I told my son to take an interest in the service academies and ROTC programs because it can be really difficult to get scholarships. I think it's best to tailor your choices towards what you can afford.

—JORDAN CASELL
STAFFORD, VIRGINIA
🎓 1

I LEARNED A REALLY HELPFUL TIP IN A SEMINAR. The speaker said that if you get accepted to your first-choice college but get a better financial offer from one of your other choices, you should use the other offer to try to get more money from your first choice. He told us to write a letter to our first choice, include a copy of the financial offer from the other school, and explain that you would prefer to go to the school you are writing to but would like them to match the financial offer from the other school. He told us that 95 percent of the time the school you want to attend will give you the extra money.

Consider

—LAURA
ESCONDIDO, CALIFORNIA
🎓 1
🏛 UNIVERSITY OF ARIZONA

• • • • • • • •

THERE ARE LOTS OF LITTLE-KNOWN SCHOLARSHIPS out there if you know where to look, but sometimes you have to position yourself to take advantage of them. Get your grandfather or parents to join organizations like the American Legion, which have scholarships for the grand-children and children of members. An American Legion member told me that they average less than five applicants a year for a scholarship for Eagle Scouts who are children and grandchildren of active, dues-paying members.

—RICHARD TYLER
REDMOND, WASHINGTON
🎓 1
🏛 NEW MEXICO INSTITUTE OF MINING & TECHNOLOGY

A WAY TO FIGURE IT OUT

If you need financial aid, search for schools that have large endowments. When I searched for colleges to suggest to my kids, I looked for schools that gave financial aid to at least 80 percent of their students. Then I told my kids that I would pay for the cost of a state education; anything over that they would have to pick up. Both of my kids are at private schools and we received aid to pay for half of the tuitions at both schools, which is only a couple of thousand dollars above the cost of our state schools. Our kids both took out loans for the amount they went over. I think, in the end, my husband and I will pay the loans for them. For now though, it is important for them to have a stake in their education because I think they respect anything they pay for themselves just a little bit more.

—KATHIE
COOPERSBURG, PENNSYLVANIA
2
PRINCIPIA COLLEGE; ROANOKE COLLEGE

IF, LIKE MOST OF US MERE MORTALS, you haven't saved nearly enough money to put Sally Jo or Jim Bob through a four-year college or university, you will have to scramble to come up with the funds. Luckily, one of the best programs out there is the PLUS loan. It is a loan for parents, not students, with a relatively low interest rate. The loan is a good way to get your child started if you don't have the funds to do it. We opted to use a PLUS loan for the first year and the following years were paid for by cashing out equity in our home. This worked for us but isn't something that would necessarily work for everyone. We were lucky enough to have a boatload of equity in our house.

—ANNETTE
GERMANTOWN, MARYLAND
2
JAMES MADISON UNIVERSITY;
UNIVERSITY OF MARYLAND, COLLEGE PARK

. . . .

Apply online to as many of your schools as you can. That way you don't have to pay an application fee. It was quick and saved us a bundle of money.

—MONA GLOVER
CINCINNATI, OHIO
1
KENYON COLLEGE

WHEN MY DAUGHTER BEGAN LOOKING at colleges her guidance counselor advised her not to limit her search of schools based on affordability. Big mistake! The counselor led her to believe that it's worth applying to expensive private schools that offer no need-based assistance because, well … you never know! Maybe she thought we might win the lottery or receive an inheritance from a rich relative. Perhaps the counselor's motto is, "Where there's a will, there's a way." Unfortunately, we adopted this motto due to our daughter's stellar academic performance, which we assumed would bring some financial relief. Little did we know that many of the more prestigious schools do not provide financial assistance based on merit.

—ANONYMOUS
EASTON, PENNSYLVANIA
🎓 1
🏫 TUFTS UNIVERSITY

> *When you visit some colleges—usu ally small, private ones—they will waive the applica- tion fee.*
>
> —REBECCA YOUNG
> TACOMA,
> WASHINGTON

· · · · · · · ·

EVERY SCHOOL WE VISITED PROMISED THE WORLD. They lectured to a large group of parents about how much money was available and how they would give you a large amount of it. One school claimed they give out $30 million in scholarships. My girls were A students in high school and we didn't get any aid, so I wonder exactly who is getting all of this aid?

—J.H.
PASADENA, CALIFORNIA
🎓 2
🏫 UNIVERSITY OF SOUTHERN CALIFORNIA

A LOT OF SMALL, PRIVATE SCHOOLS offer merit-based scholarships to good students, which helps defray tuition costs. Don't be afraid to ask about that, and then be proactive! Once we started getting scholarship offers, we went back and asked if they could be increased at all. We weren't shy about asking for more and the schools often came back with it. Some people might think what they offer is all you can get. But if that school really wants your child to come there, they'll do what they can to get him.

—MONA GLOVER
CINCINNATI, OHIO
1
KENYON COLLEGE

• • • • • • • •

MY DAUGHTER IS PRETTY SPOILED. She's never lacked anything and not because I have a lot of money, but because I wanted her to have a good life. Now that she is in college, I can't afford to give her everything, and it was really hard to explain things to her. I actually had to sit down and have a serious conversation with her, because all her life she thought we had a lot of money. She was pretty surprised to hear the truth about our finances. I sometimes wish I hadn't put up such a front for her in order to make her believe that we were very secure.

—JANET
LAS VEGAS, NEVADA
1
UNIVERSITY OF ARIZONA

KEEP AN OPEN MIND

College is an investment you and your child are making in his future, and with planning and an open-minded approach, you can figure out a comfortable solution. Do not be scared of private schools without first doing some research. Financial aid can make a private school as cheap as a public school, and there are many types of financial assistance. "Elite" schools should only be considered elite for their high admissions standards, not for their student populations. The top schools are making concerted efforts to court the top achievers regardless of income—especially those needing strong financial assistance. This is very good news. Financial planning and years of family belt-tightening are likely to be in order, but in many places, your only limitations to admission are your students' dreams.

MY SON'S GRANDFATHER LEFT MONEY in a trust for college tuition and lodging. I paid for all of the living expenses. I didn't want my son to get a job while he was in college, because he worked so hard to get good grades. I asked my son for a budget and discussed finances with him. He had a very strict budget, more strict than I would have planned for him. I gave him extra, his aunt sent him money and so did his grandmother. His aunt gave him a gas card. His dad and I split the cost of a car for him.

—DEE DEE MELMET
REDWOOD CITY, CALIFORNIA
🦉 1
🏛 NORTHERN ARIZONA UNIVERSITY

• • • • • • • • •

MAKE SURE THAT YOU GET all of your financial forms in with your applications. After my son was rejected at Yale for early decision, we were certain that he would also be rejected from Duke, so we didn't send in certain supplemental financial information that was requested. But guess what? He was accepted to Duke University and there we were with an acceptance letter from the school of my son's dreams, but no financial aid package to go along with it.

—BERURAH RUNYON
DERBY, KANSAS
🦉 1
🏛 DUKE UNIVERSITY

WHEN WE APPLIED TO COLLEGES for financial aid, they said that my son had to contribute 35 percent of his savings to his education, while I only had to contribute five percent of my savings. When I found this out, I told my mother to stop contributing money to my son's account. If I knew that early on, I would have just saved money for my son's education in my own account.

—JILLIAN
OAKLAND, CALIFORNIA
🎓 1
🏛 CALIFORNIA INSTITUTE OF TECHNOLOGY

• • • • • • • • •

MY SON GRADUATED AT THE TOP of his class in high school and scored really well on his college entrance exams, so he had a lot of choices when he applied to college. We told him that we would support his choice, no matter where or how expensive it was. Ultimately, he decided to go to the school that offered him the best aid package. He was accepted to more prestigious schools that were not as generous, but he assured us that his success in life was not directly related to the college he attended. He said he couldn't go if he knew that we were overextending ourselves just for him. My son actually taught me a lesson in life: it's true, there is a school for everyone, and you don't have to go to the one that is ranked number one by some magazine in order to do well in life.

—J.M.
RENO, NEVADA
🎓 1
🏛 UNIVERSITY OF PENNSYLVANIA

HARVARD AND OTHER PRESTIGIOUS East Coast schools are really expensive and it's not just tuition, room and board; it's all of the extras. My son goes there on scholarship and we still can't afford it. He's a senior now and he resents us a bit for sending him to a school where rich people surround him. He can't keep up with his friends who vacation all over the world, shop at the finest stores and seem to have a lot of extra money to spend on leisure activities.

> —ANONYMOUS
> LAS VEGAS, NEVADA
> 1
> HARVARD UNIVERSITY

• • • • • • • •

I WORKED OUT A DEAL WITH MY DAUGHTERS before they started school. I told them that I would pay their tuition and related expenses and they would have to pay their room and board. I told them that they could either take out loans or work as resident advisors to cover their room and board. College is a whole package, and you don't want to do everything for them. They need to learn to live independently and I don't have a problem with making them shoulder just a little bit of the burden.

> —J.H.
> PASADENA, CALIFORNIA
> 2
> UNIVERSITY OF SOUTHERN CALIFORNIA

Before you even think about college, have your child take the PSAT to try to qualify as a National Merit Scholar.

> —CAMILLE
> CINCINNATI,
> OHIO
> UNIVERSITY
> OF KENTUCKY

DON'T LET YOUR KIDS APPLY to schools that you can't afford. A lot of our friends just let their kids apply anywhere, and of course their kids got into some really expensive schools and immediately set their sights on those high-priced campuses. We had friends who used their retirement savings to keep their kids happy, and I think that is foolish. I told my daughter that the most we would be able to afford was one of our state schools. She did want to apply to some private schools so I told her very clearly that if she decided to go to a private school she wouldn't be able to go unless she got merit-based aid, and even with that, she would probably have to get a job. She ended up at a state school. She is a junior now and is very happy.

—KAREN
SCOTTSDALE, ARIZONA
🎓 1
🏛 UNIVERSITY OF ARIZONA

• • • • • • • •

We'll have kids in college for seven years, so we made sure to buy two decent vehicles that would last at least that long with no car payments.

—V.A.
AUSTIN, TEXAS
🎓 2
🏛 RICE UNIVERSITY; UNIVERSITY OF TEXAS, AUSTIN

THERE ARE MANY COLLEGES out there for a kid to choose from and there are scholarships galore. But they do require work on the part of the kid to get them. Your kids have to look at it as a job, since they will be paid for the work eventually.

—SHERRY APPEL
WASHINGTON, D.C.
🎓 2
🏛 JOHNSON & WALES UNIVERSITY

• • • • • • • •

MY DAUGHTER HAS A FULL RIDE to several schools but to her the opportunity to go to Notre Dame is priceless so she is willing to take on the necessary debt to pay for her education. She is applying for several scholarships and is willing to work in college and over vacations. She will graduate with about $20,000 in debt.

—KATHLEEN RIDER
HYDE PARK, NEW YORK
🎓 4
🏛 STATE UNIVERSITY OF NEW YORK (2)
FORDHAM UNIVERSITY; QUINNIPIAC UNIVERSITY

THE GOOD NEWS

Even though the acceptance rate at the most selective colleges has plummeted, the overall rate among the more than 2,500 four-year colleges and universities in the country—70 percent—hasn't changed since the 1980s.

UNLESS YOU ARE CERTAIN that you can afford it, don't apply ED to a school. My son applied this way to an Ivy League school, and was accepted. But in the end, they didn't offer enough aid, so he couldn't go. When you back out like this, no other top schools will accept you, so my son ended up spending a year at a community college before transferring to a better school.

—G.V.
HOUSTON, TEXAS
🎓 2
🏛 UNIVERSITY OF TEXAS, AUSTIN; UNIVERSITY OF MICHIGAN

• • • • • • • • •

I AM A SINGLE MOTHER and I have three children. I don't make that much money, but I own a home, so my daughter did not get as much aid as she thought she would. Someone advised me to have her call her school's financial aid office to explain our circumstances. She spoke to someone there, who advised her to write a letter and told her what she should put in the letter. I couldn't believe it, but it worked. They are not paying for everything, but at least it is manageable for me now.

—J.M.
SCOTTSDALE, ARIZONA
🎓 1
🏛 LOYOLA UNIVERSITY, NEW ORLEANS

Consider

RESEARCH, AND HEDGE YOUR BETS

How can you help direct your child to the places he will love that may provide financial support? First, it is always recommended that he apply to a state school—it's the only guarantee in these days of competitive admissions. Your child may not gain admission to the state campus he wants, but a state school is a solid, affordable home. In assessing the cost of private schools, look at financial aid and admissions statistics—how many students receive aid? What is the average award? Is there merit-based aid? If students regularly receive large amounts of aid, remember that the expensive private school can be as affordable as the state school.

There are financial aid calculators available on the Web these days where you can plug in some basic information about your financial status and get an estimate about potential aid that colleges will grant when assessing your financial situation. Preparing for the college's evaluation process by setting reasonable expectations—what is true, need-based aid, versus what you would really like—will help you manage the financial aid process.

MY HUSBAND AND I DON'T MAKE a lot of money, so we knew that we couldn't afford to pay for college without some loans. We made a decision together to take out a loan to pay for our daughter's school. We didn't think she should have to graduate with a huge financial burden. At the same time we decided that she would have to work part time to pay for incidentals while she was in school. She was upset at first, but we assured her that if it got too difficult to maintain her grades and work at the same time, we would help her out a little more to ease the stress.

—NANCY
LAS VEGAS, NEVADA
1
DUKE UNIVERSITY

· · · · · · · ·

PRIVATE SCHOOLS ARE VERY EXPENSIVE. Even if your kid is on a full scholarship, it is still hard. Your kids' friends are going on ski trips, camping trips, and lavish vacations, and you don't want to say, "No, you can't go." It's the culture there and a lot of the kids are doing it. And even if you don't send them on the trips, everything at school is expensive. It's like shopping at Macy's as opposed to Saks; you can get the same thing, but at Saks it's going to be triple the price. So if you go to Harvard, as opposed to Boston College, your dollar gets spread a lot thinner.

—HENRY NOYES
CHICAGO, ILLINOIS
2
HARVARD UNIVERSITY; WELLESLEY COLLEGE

I STARTED SAVING FOR MY DAUGHTER'S education when she was born. Then I got divorced and it became very difficult to put money aside. About four years before college I started reaching out to family members for help. Her father helped a lot, and both sets of grandparents contributed as well. I was able to put money into accounts I set up in her name, which allowed us to not pay taxes on the money.

—TRACY
CHICAGO, ILLINOIS
🎓 1
🏛 WASHINGTON UNIVERSITY

. . . .

IF YOU ARE DIVORCED AND YOUR SPOUSE is a high earner, look for schools that do not account for non-custodial income. My ex-wife is an attorney and she makes a very good living. If my daughter chose a school that looked at my ex's income, we would have never qualified for aid. So if you have this problem too, look for schools that ask how much your non-custodial spouse would be willing to contribute instead of a school that asks for their tax forms, income and assets. Most schools that just have you fill out the FAFSA only most likely won't look at your ex's income, but if you have to fill out the College Board form too, then they will probably take the spouse's income into account.

—STEPHEN
VANCOUVER, WASHINGTON
🎓 2
🏛 FURMAN UNIVERSITY; OREGON STATE UNIVERSITY

DON'T SELL YOUR OPTIONS for a free ride. My son did not apply for financial aid because we wouldn't qualify. I am paying for every last dime of my son's education and it's a stretch. But I wouldn't even think of having him apply to a school that was willing to give him a free ride where he would be bored.

—ANONYMOUS
PORTLAND, OREGON
🎓 1
🏛 STANFORD UNIVERSITY

• • • • • • • • •

WE TOLD OUR SON THAT he could apply anywhere he wanted, but when the acceptances rolled in with no financial aid from the prestigious universities, we had to tell him that he couldn't go to the school of his dreams. My son really wanted to go to Caltech, but unfortunately they barely offered him enough money to cover his meals. The only way we could have afforded to send him would have been to spend our retirement savings. This just about broke his heart. I am about to start this process with my second child now, and I've already spoken to her about how much we can afford. I've told her that she can still apply wherever she wants, but she knows that if she doesn't receive enough aid, she just can't go.

—ANONYMOUS
LOS ANGELES, CALIFORNIA
🎓 2
🏛 UNIVERSITY OF CALIFORNIA, LOS ANGELES;
UNIVERSITY OF CALIFORNIA, BERKELEY

EVEN AFTER YOUR CHILD ENROLLS, keep asking about scholarship opportunities. Once my son started his sophomore year in college, he found out his school offered returning scholarships. We had no idea they even existed, but were very happy when he got one!

—DONNA
CINCINNATI, OHIO
🎓 2
🏛 MIAMI UNIVERSITY

• • • • • • • •

YOUR CHILD SHOULD BE AWARE of how much college costs. Ask your child if s/he is ready to go to college. If they aren't ready then your best and most affordable choice would be community college. They can go for a year or two until they figure out where they want to go. It's a good option to consider for some parents!

—DIANE LANG
FLANDERS, NEW JERSEY

DATA ON DOLLARS

In the years most recently surveyed, $134 billion in financial aid has been available to college students and their families. Additionally, about 62 percent of all full-time college students receive some form of grant aid.

WE HAD SAVINGS IN COLLEGEINVEST.ORG. We also had a townhouse in the mountains and will use the proceeds from selling it as part of the educational fund.

—ANONYMOUS
HIGHLANDS RANCH, COLORADO
1

• • • • • • • •

WHEN LESS-THAN-TOP SCHOOLS offer you a free ride, it's because your kid probably has a lot to offer the school, not the other way around. I suggest applying to some good reach schools, because if your kid gets accepted to any of those, then you know that he or she will probably be bored at a lesser school.

—ANONYMOUS
CHICAGO, ILLINOIS
2
BOSTON UNIVERSITY; DUKE UNIVERSITY

ADMIT STATS

College admission for the high school class graduating in 2007 was the most selective ever, especially at the nation's top-rated colleges and universities.

Stanford accepted 10.3 percent of its applicants; Harvard, a record-setting 9 percent, the lowest rate in its history. Columbia accepted 8.9 percent of applicants, one of the lowest rates in the country.

Parent to Parent: Competition & Controversy

You figured that your child would be the anxious one about this process, but surprise—it's running your life, too! As you go to school events with other parents, socialize with work colleagues, and bump into your neighbors, you will be talking about college admissions more than you can imagine—at least for the junior and senior years of high school. It can be helpful to hear others' stories to learn about the process and avoid their mistakes, but you most certainly will hear more than you want to. It is going to scare you when you hear how well your friend's child is doing; you will automatically compare him to your child (for better or worse). With all of the pressure, you may find yourself competing with your peers. There is, additionally, the veiled threat that your friends' children are applying to the same schools as your child, and surely, the colleges will not take every applicant from your high school. You hear about all of the things one parent is doing for her child and you start to feel that you are not doing enough for yours.

How can you manage these interactions without getting swept away? First, remember that you have no way to judge the accuracy of whatever a parent spouts: he may be exaggerating about his child's accomplishments and the schools to which he is applying. Trust that colleges will sort all of this out. Parents are biased—surprise, surprise—and the badly behaving, competitive parents may just be letting the pressure get to them. You want to be the parent who is gracefully rising above the stress. Remind yourself that most parents are not admissions officers; they have no real way of knowing how colleges make decisions. You can discount any comments from people who "know" their kids will be admitted to a favorite college. Take the competitive rhetoric and laugh it off. Keep your eye on the real prize—the right match for your child.

THERE IS THIS FRENZY GOING ON in upper-class neighbor-hoods. It's like a new sport called, Where Is Your Kid Applying? The parents get caught up in it; the kids don't, or if they do, they internalize it. What amazed me was how obsessive the whole thing was. We would go to football games on Friday nights at my son's high school and all the parents would sit there with their notes and talk about who was applying where, who got in where and what would give your kid an edge. I never thought I would get caught up in it, but I did.

—MARYANNE LAGUARDIA
SANTA MONICA, CALIFORNIA
2
BELOIT COLLEGE; UNIVERSITY OF ARIZONA

• • • • • • • • •

I DIDN'T HAVE THAT MUCH TO DO with the college admissions process. I told my daughters to make sure they knew all of the deadlines. They asked me for the application fees and I paid all of them. We sent both of them on college tours. One daughter went on a high school trip to visit colleges in northern California and the other went on her own to visit one of the schools she applied to. I think it's good for them to do all of that on their own because it is an essential part of preparing them to be on their own.

—ANTHONY ROMANO
SAN DIEGO, CALIFORNIA
2
UNIVERSITY OF CALIFORNIA, SAN DIEGO;
CLAREMONT MCKENNA COLLEGE

OH, THOSE KIDS

My daughter came home from school one day and said her friend applied to 28 schools. I said to my daughter, "That's crazy. No family in its right mind is going to cough up 50 to 75 dollars a pop for 28 schools. She's probably just saying that because you only applied to one and she's just trying to get a rise out of you." Well, three days later I'm in the art supply store and there is that girl with her mom. I thought, "OK, I'm taking her down."

I walked straight over to them, all fired up, and I said, "My kid tells me you applied to 28 schools. Come on, for real: How many did you apply to?" The mother looked me straight in the eye and said, "My daughter applied to 28 schools." She said her daughter just couldn't make a decision. I think she was embarrassed, and then I was embarrassed.

This girl did really well in school. But she ended up going to a sub-par state school to be with her boyfriend, while my daughter ended up at her first-choice school. I guess you could say it was the ultimate equalizer.

—Terry
Irvine, California
1
Mount Holyoke College

MY DAUGHTER GOES TO A WEST LOS ANGELES prep school, and the peer pressure to do well and prepare is intense. And as a parent, there is pressure too. It's subtle. For example, I know a lot of her friends are applying to top schools, and for years their parents have been enrolling them in classes and clubs that would look good on their college applications. I don't believe in that. Everyone is constantly talking about college and where their kids are going. I just ignore the other parents and I am secure in knowing that whatever happens will be for the best. I truly believe that regardless of where my daughter goes to college, she will do well in life.

—VICKI
LOS ANGELES, CALIFORNIA
♟ 2
🏛 CALIFORNIA STATE UNIVERSITY, NORTHRIDGE; UNDECIDED

• • • • • • • •

HOW MUCH SHOULD YOU BE HELPING? A lot. This is the real world and not a time to suddenly get too squishy on the ethics issue. You should not do any of the application work for your child for a number of reasons, including the fact that admissions officers can spot that a mile away. But you can review with him/her what the most appropriate essay topic is, point the student in the right direction, and suggest some edits.

—EDWARD HERSHEY
PORTLAND, OREGON
♟ 3
🏛 CORNELL UNIVERSITY (2), COLORADO COLLEGE

IF YOU WILL BE SENDING YOUR KIDS to private college, make sure you have a talk with them about what to expect in terms of the people they will come across who have obscene amounts of money. I had some serious talks with my daughter about the fact that she was going to run into people with a lot more money than we have and that she might at times feel pressure to conform to certain things. I think you just want them to be aware, so when they get there, they don't feel left out.

—STEPHEN
VANCOUVER, WASHINGTON
2
FURMAN UNIVERSITY; OREGON STATE UNIVERSITY

• • • • • • • •

We live in a very competitive town. Parents are always trying to outdo each other. I felt that if we didn't spend a lot of money on a private college advisor, the other kids would have an advantage over mine.

—KAREN
SCOTTSDALE, ARIZONA
1
UNIVERSITY OF ARIZONA

IT'S HARD ON THE PARENTS

When my daughter was applying to college, a lot of our close friends were parents of kids of the same age. It was amazing how competitive and how charged the energy was around grades and scores. I can't say that I didn't get caught up in it. I tried not to, but it really affected friendships temporarily. When my daughter was rejected from Stanford it was actually almost embarrassing. Other parents were bragging about their kids, and if your kid didn't get into her top choice it was somehow a reflection on you, the parent. It's really hard not to get into the competing aspect. I don't think we ever viewed each other as enemies, but what we tended to do was project ourselves onto our children and to see their accomplishments or lack there of as our own. As you are getting older and you are settled in your career and you are not achieving great things anymore, you sort of absorb your children's achievements as your own. You have to work really hard to not see what they are doing as your own goal and accomplishment.

—KAREN BARCHAS
TRUCKEE, CALIFORNIA
♀ 1
🏛 UNIVERSITY OF CALIFORNIA, BERKELEY

VIEW OTHER PARENTS AS ALLIES and a wonderful source of information during this confusing time. Try to network and "pay it forward" to get through the process. When our daughter was in her junior year, I tapped into our neighbor's experience of getting her first child into college. During my daughter's freshman year of college, another neighbor who was just embarking on the process told me how confused she was. I happily helped her through the process with my experience and any resources we had in our home. We all have a common concern—our children—and this should not be a competition.

—ANONYMOUS
KENT, WASHINGTON
2
WASHINGTON STATE UNIVERSITY; UNIVERSITY OF WASHINGTON

• • • • • • • •

I WOULD TELL ANY PARENT who is forcing their kid to apply to a certain school to back off unless there is a financial reason. My son's guidance counselors wanted to make sure we knew that with my son's grades and scores he could be a candidate at the Ivies, but he just wasn't interested. We did make him visit the various campuses, but when he showed no interest, we let him make his own decision about where he wanted to go.

—ANONYMOUS
RICHMOND, VIRGINIA
1
UNIVERSITY OF VIRGINIA

When my son was in the eighth grade, I spoke to some seniors who had just gotten into the top schools and got their input on the best path to take.

—ANONYMOUS
PITTSBURGH, PENNSYLVANIA
CORNELL UNIVERSITY

THERE ARE A LOT OF WEB SITES out there aimed at college students and their parents. It's a great way to connect with other people who are going through the same things that you are. You get so many different perspectives from people in other parts of the country, with different socio-economic status and just totally different ideas. Put yourself out there and don't be afraid to ask questions; you will get a lot in return. The one thing you must have is a thick skin, since lots of people on the site are quick to criticize. Just ignore the instigators and don't engage them.

—BERURAH RUNYON
DERBY, KANSAS
🎓 1
🏛 DUKE UNIVERSITY

• • • • • • • • •

I WAS NOT INVOLVED AT ALL in my son's application process. A lot of my friends were constantly commenting to me, "Did you go to this meeting? Did you hire someone to help with the applications? Aren't you reading over your son's essay?" The list goes on. I know my son can handle anything on his own. He didn't need me. So every time a parent tried to assert some authority over me, my stock answer was, "My son is valedictorian; he's already proven that he can do it on his own."

—ANONYMOUS
LAS VEGAS, NEVADA
🎓 1
🏛 HARVARD UNIVERSITY

I THOUGHT THAT VOLUNTEERING at my son's high school would give me a little edge over other parents in terms of needing things from advisors and teachers at the high school. I didn't set out to volunteer with that goal in mind, but as I spent more time and got to know the principal and the advisors, I realized that I could use the newly formed relationships to my advantage. I feel that when they do things for him, like write recommendations or get his transcripts out, they know me and might use a bit more care.

—L.R.
SCOTTSDALE, ARIZONA
🎓 1
🏛 UNIVERSITY OF CALIFORNIA, BERKELEY

• • • • • • • • •

CALLING OTHER PARENTS AND ASKING for advice is a great way to get information, but think about whom you're asking and what kind of position you're putting them in. People who have already been through the whole college process were more than happy to tell me things and give me advice, but it's a different story for other parents who are still in the middle of it all. There are just so many spots and scholarships to go around, especially from any particular high school, so it's understandable if those people don't want to give out too much information—and you shouldn't feel pressured to, either.

—CAMILLE
CINCINNATI, OHIO
🎓 1
🏛 UNIVERSITY OF KENTUCKY

A HELPFUL PARENT . . .

- Asks his child his dreams and listens to him;

- Attends high school presentations and guidance counselor meetings (where appropriate);

- Assesses his own selfish needs and tries to separate them from his child's;

- Puts together a list of possible schools, insuring that his child will have several good places for himself;

- Visits schools (where possible);

- Helps plan essays to help his child highlight his strengths;

- Pushes his child to work hard, but celebrates his hard work;

- Insists that his child run the admissions process (i.e., call admissions officers and write e-mails to them directly).

WE HAD A GOOD RELATIONSHIP with other parents during the application process. We are not engineers and, since my son was applying for engineering, we went to parents who were engineers for advice. And we gave them advice in our field of work—health care.

—ANONYMOUS
PITTSBURGH, PENNSYLVANIA
🎓 1
🏫 CORNELL UNIVERSITY

• • • • • • • •

I WAS EXCITED THAT MY DAUGHTER was accepted into all the colleges of her choice, but she expected to visit every last one of them to make her final decision. She told me how her best friend's parents were visiting at least eight schools. I thought looking at the brochures was enough for making decisions. But her friend's parents took her along on three trips, which hurt my feelings a little.

—ANONYMOUS
CHICAGO, ILLINOIS
🎓 1
🏫 SOUTHERN ILLINOIS UNIVERSITY; WESTERN ILLINOIS UNIVERSITY

• • • • • • • •

I LEARNED A LOT FROM GOING through the process with my daughter and learned that I shouldn't have been as involved and frenetic as I was with her. I didn't write my daughter's essays or anything like that, but I sat with her while she was filling out her applications. I hovered.

—KAREN BARCHAS
TRUCKEE, CALIFORNIA
🎓 1
🏫 UNIVERSITY OF CALIFORNIA, BERKELEY

A HARMFUL PARENT . . .

- Puts his needs first and makes this process about himself;

- Fills out forms for his child;

- Writes the essays for his child;

- Pressures his child to gain admission to a specific school;

- Contacts the universities about the applications because his child is "too busy";

- Abdicates responsibility in the process and puts it all on his child;

- Argues with the guidance counselor and the high school;

- Blames failure on his child and not on the process.

A **LOT OF PEOPLE GET TUNNEL VISION** and can't see past
Harvard, Yale and Princeton. Popular culture is all about
certain colleges. The man on the street knows about
Harvard, Yale, and Princeton, but there are so many mag-
nificent schools out there that are just below everyone's
radar. Do not dismiss the opportunities they can provide
for your child.

—TOM
WACO, TEXAS
1
RHODES COLLEGE

Tests:
Not Just
a Number

One of the last admissions factors within your child's power is his test scores. For some students, a lot of extra help may be required to succeed in this area. Preparing for the tests—with test-preparation courses, private tutoring, and simply studying—becomes an extracurricular activity of its own. Starting in 10th grade with the PSAT or PACT, your child will get some indication of how well he tests. This may be great news, or notification that he'll need to make time for a new after-school activity.

How can you tell how high your child needs to score? You can surf Web sites to get a sense of the range of test scores of admitted students at a particular college and figure out where your child fits according to those statistics. Your child should score at least in the middle of the pack for a school that he may want to go to.

Schools love to see an applicant's grades match his test scores. After that, they prefer students with high GPAs and lower test scores to those with weak grades and high scores (which indicates the students are not performing to potential, possibly, on a daily basis). So, the test score is never the final criterion of an application.

How do you decide if you should get help for your child? These days it seems almost a given that families enroll their children in some sort of test preparation course. But this is a very individual process and your child may or may not need to engage in extensive preparation. Yes, there are "tricks" of sorts to the tests, but test scores tend not to go up 300 points, despite what the courses proclaim, unless something radical changes in a student's life. Cramming does not usually work—reading, and really learning, throughout high school does. Think of the test-prep classes and individual study as medicine, but not a cure.

MY DAUGHTER TOOK HER FIRST SAT without much preparation and she did well, but not well enough to get into
some of the selective schools. For the second time I
bought the College Board book and asked her to read it.
Then I gave her a few practice tests where I proctored for
her. I wanted to simulate the real testing environment for
her. Take a Saturday morning and sit at the dining room
table with your stopwatch. I timed each section, and after
she was done we sat together and went over the results
and the explanations. I talked them through with her
using the book. She took the SAT, and her scores went
up 140 points. She was happy.

—PETER
SEATTLE, WASHINGTON
🎓 1
🏫 SWARTHMORE COLLEGE

• • • • • • • • •

THE SAT AND ACT TEST PREP classes can be a very
worthwhile investment. My daughter didn't take them,
but my son did, and it made a difference in his scores
when he retook the test. Higher test scores can really
make a difference with the scholarship money they're
able to get, so the classes pretty much pay for themselves.

—JENNIFER
CINCINNATI, OHIO
🎓 1
🏫 MIAMI UNIVERSITY OF OHIO

WE SIGNED UP OUR DAUGHTER for every SAT review course under the sun. We had to stay on top of her to make sure she went to the classes because she didn't like them. We actually would bribe her to go to classes: we would take her to her favorite restaurant, buy her the shirt she wanted, and so forth. It was all worth it: she took the SAT three times and the difference in her score from the first time to the third was over 250 points.

> —NANCY
> LAS VEGAS, NEVADA
> ☗ 1
> ⚏ DUKE UNIVERSITY

• • • • • • • • •

UNLESS YOU HAVE A CHILD that has some intrinsic motivation, don't push too hard when it comes to tests like the SAT. I had my son take his PSAT without studying just to get a baseline to know where he was and if there was need for improvement. I wanted him to take a class, but I knew he wasn't motivated and it would be a waste of time. The first time he took the SAT, he did well, but was frustrated because he didn't do as well as some of his friends. That's what motivated him; before the second time around, he sat and did some practice tests and his scores improved.

> —C.K.
> LARKSPUR, CALIFORNIA
> ☗ 1
> ⚏ WHITMAN COLLEGE

PSAT 411

NO ONE TELLS YOU THAT THE PSAT is what determines whether or not your kid makes National Merit Scholar. My oldest missed being a National Merit semifinalist by two points on the math section of her PSAT. If I had known that it meant so much, I would have pushed.

> —T.M.
> SAN FRANCISCO, CALIFORNIA
> 1
> UNDECIDED

* * * * * * * *

MOST PEOPLE THINK THAT THE PSATS are just for practice; they are not. Your score on them determines whether or not you can be a semi-finalist for a National Merit Scholar award. I learned after my first child to have a very healthy respect for the National Merit Scholar Award. If your kids score in the top five percent on the PSAT, then they automatically become semi-finalists. My first son qualified without studying, but only because I had no idea that the PSAT was for anything but practice for the SAT. But when it came time for my second son to take his PSAT, I had him sign up with a private tutor. I don't think people realize the doors that open to you when you earn this award. Schools really want National Merit Scholars.

> —J.M.
> MARIETTA, GEORGIA
> 1
> RICE UNIVERSITY

MY DAUGHTER WAS SET on going to her first college pick. However, the college required a 24 or better on the ACTs. My daughter studied hard and got a 20. She was angry for a couple of days because it meant she was going to miss the first college application deadline. For the second test she studied all night, every night, for a month. She still got a 20. The disappointment on her face made me want to stay away from the house. She told me she was still going to apply to her favorite school, even though she was past the deadline and only received a 20. I still believed in her because she believed in herself. She was rejected. I think I was hurt more than she was.

—KEVIN ITSON
CHICAGO, ILLINOIS
1
UNIVERSITY OF ILLINOIS, URBANA-CHAMPAIGN

• • • • • • • •

One of my daughters took the SAT once, and the other took it twice. One of them said to me, "I'm happy with my scores." I said, "If you are happy, then I am happy."

—C.T.
SANTA MONICA, CALIFORNIA
2
SIMMONS COLLEGE; CORNELL UNIVERSITY

I WOULD ADVISE PARENTS TO INSIST that their child sub-scribe to Word of the Day (free) or SAT Prep Question of the Day (also free), or some sort of daily info like those. Mind you, my kids never did ... but that's what I would advise. We used private tutors who were also, in my opin-ion, mostly coaches of the psyche. Expensive, but a must!

—MIRIAM SILVERMAN
ELKINS PARK, PENNSYLVANIA
[#KIDS IN COLLEGE] 2
SYRACUSE UNIVERSITY; UNIVERSITY OF MARYLAND

• • • • • • • •

I BOUGHT ONE OF THOSE CDS with practice tests on it. Both of my kids took the ACT a couple of times, and they both raised their scores after using the CD. With my daughter, especially, the higher score made a differ-ence in the number of scholarships she was offered, so the $40 I spent on it was worth its weight in gold.

Consider

—REBECCA TOMAN
CANFIELD, OHIO
2
UNIVERSITY OF CINCINNATI; XAVIER UNIVERSITY

• • • • • • • •

MY DAUGHTER HAD ACCESS to an online SAT program at school but she didn't take advantage of it. She took the SAT cold the first time and didn't do as well as she wanted to. We hired a tutor and her score increased substantially the second time she took it.

—T.W.
LITHONIA, GEORGIA
1

MISTAKES WERE MADE

MY DAUGHTER TOOK THE SAT TWICE. The second time, her math score had dropped by about 100 points! We knew that was just too drastic, so we got in touch with the College Board to ask them to recalculate the score by hand. We had to wait for request forms and then fill them out, mail them back, *and* pay 50 dollars on top of it. When they finally recounted and sent the correct score, the wrong ones had already been sent out to the colleges she'd applied to. It took two months to get everything straightened out.

—D.J.S.
EASTON, PENNSYLVANIA
🦷 1
🏛 TUFTS UNIVERSITY

• • • • • • • •

THE SECOND TIME MY SON TOOK THE SAT, he had dropped over 200 points in one of the sections. I thought, "This is weird. Something is wrong." I requested the actual test. We found out there was a glitch in the grading, and we had his score fixed. Don't be afraid to request the backup that shows what questions were missed. At the very least, you can see where the student might have issues or problems.

—ANONYMOUS
BROOKLYN, NEW YORK
🦷 1
🏛 BROWN UNIVERSITY

WE DIDN'T SIGN UP OUR DAUGHTERS for any expensive SAT prep classes, nor did we hire expensive tutors. I don't think it is necessary. One expensive class or tutor is not going to replace years of study time in school. Our high school offered some classes and my daughters went to them. I think the most important thing is for your kids to be well read and they will do fine. Both of my daughters did well enough to get into the schools of their choice.

—LAURA ROMANO
SAN DIEGO, CALIFORNIA
🎓 2
🏛 UNIVERSITY OF CALIFORNIA, SAN DIEGO;
CLAREMONT MCKENNA COLLEGE

* * * * * * * *

MY SON STARTED PREPARING for the SAT in ninth grade by taking practice exams. He took one at home about once a month, and with my help we simulated the testing environment as best as we could. When it came time to take the actual test, it was a breeze for him, and he only had to take it once. I really believe that this was a great way to prepare; no cramming, just part of a routine.

—J.M.
RENO, NEVADA
🎓 1
🏛 UNIVERSITY OF PENNSYLVANIA

* * * * * * * *

JUST HAVE THEM do lots of practice tests. It's the best way.

—N.
NEW YORK, NEW YORK
🎓 1
🏛 CARLETON COLLEGE

MY DAUGHTER NEVER BELIEVED IN SATs as an accurate measurement of intelligence, so she was morally against taking them. Instead of going to bed early the night before the exam, she went out and partied with her friends. She was out so late that she overslept and missed her test. Fortunately she had time to take it again. She ended up scoring well enough to get into the school she wanted to go to, so I was happy.

—JANET
LAS VEGAS, NEVADA
🎓 1
🏛 UNIVERSITY OF ARIZONA

* * * * * * * *

I FOLLOWED MY SON IN MY OWN CAR when he went to take his SAT and his ACT. I was motivated to do this by the instructors in his prep class who told us stories of what could go wrong. For example, kids get lost, get distracted, get flat tires, etc. What concerned me the most was a story about a girl who was killed in a car accident on her way to take the SAT. So I followed him to the testing center and he didn't mind at all. I would follow him into the parking lot and wave and he would carefully wave back while making sure his friends didn't see.

—ANONYMOUS
🎓 2
🏛 PRINCETON UNIVERSITY; UNIVERSITY OF PENNSYLVANIA

I AM SO UPSET, MY TEST SCORE WAS ONLY ...

The dreaded tests: torture devices that require preparation and retakes and drive your child crazy with constant thoughts of "Can I do better?" With testing, there is a ceiling. Yes, preparation will make a difference, but at some point, your child's score is really in the ballpark it will remain; future scores will only move around in insignificant tens of points. When your child reaches this point, ease the pressure on both of you. Remember, test scores are not solely based on intellect. They are influenced by income level, ethnic background, high school strength, and learning styles and abilities or disabilities. Admissions offices consider these scores together with the academics. There are many schools for which a solid showing is all you need.

And remember this as well: Your child will not be asked his test scores ever again after this admissions process. Help him do his best, try a few times, and move forward to more critical issues.

MY EXPERIENCE WITH BOYS THAT AGE: You need to give them a little bit of pushing and guidance. They tend to be less mature. Our son hadn't done particularly well on his SATs the first time. So we enrolled him in a private SAT class. He went very regularly with a lot of pushing from us, three times a week, off and on for months. He didn't need us to convince him; he knew he needed to do well. He just needed to be prodded. He ended up doing very well, scoring in the 700s on all three sections.

—C.G.
COOPER CITY, FLORIDA
🏆 3
🏛 DUKE UNIVERSITY

• • • • • • • •

TAKE THE COURSES AND GET THE TUTORS. Your kids study for tests every week, why not know about the SAT and ACT before you take them? If the colleges are only looking at the GPA and SAT, why wouldn't you want your SAT/ACT score to be the best it can be. Retake the test if you didn't do well: my son increased his score by over 130 points.

—KATHY THOMAS
DALLAS, TEXAS
🏆 1
🏛 TEXAS CHRISTIAN UNIVERSITY

I WAS CONCERNED THAT by emphasizing the importance of scoring high on the SAT, she might start to define herself by the SAT score. And if she didn't score high enough, that might affect her self-esteem. One thing I emphasized throughout this whole process was that no matter what happened, I loved her. I wasn't going to think less of her if she scored below 700.

—SUSAN
NEW ENGLAND
🎓 1
🏛 BROWN UNIVERSITY

• • • • • • • • •

PREPARING FOR COLLEGE was an emotional time for my daughter. Tests were a big cause of this. She received a 20 on her ACTs her junior year, which angered her to the point where she almost gave up on college. Since my daughter hates rejection on all levels, she was afraid to submit applications with that score. I encouraged her to study and take it again. She did, but the second time she received a 19. She was again more furious than before. She stayed in her room about a week; you would think some boy broke her heart. I encouraged her to take it one last time. The last time, she got a 22. She was slightly happy, but her goal was at least a 25. I spent at least $300 on clothes and outings to make her feel better.

—D.C.
CHICAGO, ILLINOIS
🎓 1
🏛 SOUTHERN ILLINOIS UNIVERSITY; WESTERN ILLINOIS UNIVERSITY

ARE YOU TAKING AIM AT THE RIGHT TARGET?

How can you assess which schools are a good fit, determine safety schools, and understand what reach schools are and the odds of admission to them? Look at the data that will be considered first and foremost, along with extracurriculars, by the schools—your child's test scores and his level of academic achievement. First, you will gauge your child's general testing ability through the PSAT and PACT—tests given in the sophomore year that predict a student's SAT and ACT scores. Your child's scores may improve then, but estimate conservatively. Schools at which your student falls into the middle range of testing will be solid possibilities. Otherwise, they are reaches. Second, understand your child's GPA and course load. Admission to top schools will require the most rigorous course load available at your high school as well as top grades in those courses. Test scores may be high, but if the GPA and course load is not in the same range, a school is a reach for sure.

The Grand Tours: Visiting Colleges

Without question, the best way to understand what a school is all about is to visit. Poring over Web pages and rankings and listening to stories about schools can only tell you so much—there are intangibles at each school that make it unique, and no school is really the same as another. Thus, it is critical to visit schools before you make a final decision. You and your child will be able to get a feel for the atmosphere beyond the sales materials, and after a few visits, it will become clear when a school feels "right."

To give yourself and your child the best opportunities to under-stand the wide variety of atmospheres, visit a variety of schools as well as ones your child thinks are interesting. For example, consider visiting both large and small schools—one kind will feel better for your child. Keep an open mind: you might be surprised at the schools you think you all will love, but that you actually dislike.

The smartest parents will be good listeners and observers as well as inquirers. Ask the questions you need answered, but try not to sweat the small stuff. The quality of dorms, for example, should not be the most consuming item on the tour. You should be taking note of the general way the campus takes care of itself, but your child will ultimately not love or hate a school based on something like the dorm bathrooms. Pay attention to the cues your child gives you about his level of interest in a particular school.

If you are unable to visit campuses before applying because of a lack of time or money, do not worry. Your child can apply sight-unseen and easily be admitted to a match school. Just be sure that before locking your child and yourself into a four-year emotional and financial commitment, you check out how a school feels, beyond its name. Trust yourself and his observations, and you should succeed.

THE FIRST TIME WE WENT ON TOURS was the summer after his sophomore year. We didn't have a definitive list of schools at that point, but I wanted him to get a feel for what was out there, because you just never know. The next summer, we had a concrete list of schools that he thought he would want to apply to, so we planned to visit these schools over a week.

> —JILLIAN
> OAKLAND, CALIFORNIA
> 🎓 1
> 🏛 CALIFORNIA INSTITUTE OF TECHNOLOGY

· · · · · · · · ·

MY SON WENT ON COLLEGE TOURS with his friends from high school, while my daughter went with her mother. I think they both went about it in the right way. You just have to know your children. My son is independent and my daughter asks her mother for advice at every turn, so I knew it would be helpful for my daughter to have her mother there.

> —ANONYMOUS
> LAS VEGAS, NEVADA
> 🎓 1
> 🏛 HARVARD UNIVERSITY

· · · · · · · · ·

IF YOU ARE GOING TO VISIT A CAMPUS, make sure classes will be in session before you plan your trip.

> —J.M.
> SCOTTSDALE, ARIZONA
> 🎓 1
> 🏛 LOYOLA UNIVERSITY NEW ORLEANS

TOO MUCH INFORMATION?

When we went on the tour for Tufts, my daughter had already been accepted, so it was her second visit to the campus. The rest of the group was made up of high school juniors and their parents. The student guide must have made a dozen references to what she considered the college's major draw: "great parties," including an annual naked quad run, where hundreds of students rip off their clothes and run bare-assed across the campus! She felt compelled to share that she had participated in her sophomore year, prompting a visual I did not want to visualize!

Because we had seen the campus before, and had gotten lots of input about the academic environment, we knew that the school had great things to offer, but I'm pretty sure some of those other parents were mentally crossing it off the list. It's important to visit a campus more than once and to talk to staff, department heads and a variety of students to get a true reading of the school. Don't let one immature, party-happy tour guide dissuade you.

—D.J.S.
EASTON, PENNSYLVANIA
1
TUFTS UNIVERSITY

DO NOT VISIT THE COLLEGES IN THEIR PRIME weather seasons. Go to the Northeast in the dead of winter and the West Coast in the middle of summer. When we visited Amherst, it was four below zero, and the locks on the car froze shut. You want your kids to see what it is like all the time; you want them to get a real feel for the campus and what living there would be like. When my son wanted to see Harvey Mudd and Caltech, we went during the summer so he would know how hot it would be most of the time.

—J.M.
MARIETTA, GEORGIA
1
RICE UNIVERSITY

• • • • • • • •

WE USED THE SUMMER before my daughters' senior years to visit campuses. My strategy was to group the schools that they were interested in into geographical areas, and then organized two to three trips spaced throughout the summer, with each trip covering two to four schools. The planning took a considerable amount of organization— you have to figure out driving time and where you will be staying, sign up for the campus tour and interview, and map out your route between colleges. The actual visits to the campuses are fun, but also exhausting. You have to plan well and know your limitations.

—LUCY RUMACK
BROOKLYN, NEW YORK
1
SWARTHMORE COLLEGE

> *There is no reason not to apply to schools without visiting if they look like a match.*
>
> —ANONYMOUS
> PENNSYLVANIA
> ROANOKE COLLEGE;
> PRINCIPIA COLLEGE

MY DAUGHTER WENT WITH AN ORGANIZED GROUP to visit college campuses. I would have liked to go with her to see the culture at each campus. As far as her needing Mom to tag along; I did not think that was necessary. My wanting to go with her was more about my need to have her need me, and I don't think it is fair to place that burden on your children. I know we all want to spend as much time with them as possible, but the truth is that they are going to be on their own in college, so why not get them used to it?

—TRACY
CHICAGO, ILLINOIS
🎓 1
🏛 WASHINGTON UNIVERSITY

It is really important to visit a lot of schools if you can, and visit them early. We planned our first trip at the start of my daughter's junior year in high school.

—JANE
SCOTTSDALE, ARIZONA
🎓 1
🏛 UNIVERSITY OF MIAMI

I GAVE MY KIDS A LITTLE SPIRAL NOTEBOOK, and as we were leaving each college I made them pull it out and write down what they liked about it and what they didn't like, as well as what kind of overall feeling the place gave them. You'll never remember the feeling you got at each college unless you put down your thoughts and feelings then and there. If you sit down four or six months later, you'll lose all the little details that could be important. We referred to that book a lot!

> —REBECCA TOMAN
> CANFIELD, OHIO
> 🎓 2
> 🏛 UNIVERSITY OF CINCINNATI; XAVIER UNIVERSITY

• • • • • • • •

WE TOOK MY DAUGHTER ON COLLEGE visits the summer before her senior year and made a family vacation out of it. We camped along the way, stopped at local parks, and tried local restaurants. Yes, it's a serious time to gather information, but it should be enjoyable, too.

> —V.A.
> AUSTIN, TEXAS
> 🎓 2
> 🏛 RICE UNIVERSITY; UNIVERSITY OF TEXAS, AUSTIN

• • • • • • • •

IF THE WEATHER WAS BAD on the day of the visit, my daughter crossed the school right off her list.

> —N.
> NEW YORK, NEW YORK
> 🎓 1
> 🏛 CARLETON COLLEGE

LAST SPRING BREAK, my husband, my daughter, and I piled in the car, drove up to northern California and worked our way down the state, stopping at colleges along the way. I'm really glad we did it, because it's probably the last time we'll get to spend so much quality time with our daughter.

—VICKI
LOS ANGELES, CALIFORNIA
2
CALIFORNIA STATE UNIVERSITY, NORTHRIDGE; UNDECIDED

• • • • • • • • •

WHEN SCHEDULING CAMPUS TOURS, try to visit the colleges when they're in session. That way, you get a real feel for the atmosphere, the pace and the people. My husband actually stopped people walking around on campus and asked them how they liked the school. My daughter was cringing, but you can't get that kind of information from an official tour guide.

—LESLIE KUHLMAN
CINCINNATI, OHIO
1
FRANCISCAN UNIVERSITY OF STEUBENVILLE

• • • • • • • • •

MAKE SURE YOU EAT A MEAL ON CAMPUS. Food quality will be surprisingly important to your child's college experience!

—GRETA TAYLOR
BROOKLYN, NEW YORK
2
GOUCHER COLLEGE; BARD COLLEGE

Get both parents (or even another relative) to go on the college tours with your child. Three sets of ears are definitely better than one.

—MONA GLOVER
CINCINNATI, OHIO
KENYON COLLEGE

STUDENT TOUR GUIDE REVEALS ALL!

Visits are very important for what they betray about a place. The student guide at Skidmore absolutely turned us off the place when we toured with my daughter some years ago. Is that entirely rational? Could a better guide have given us a better impression? No and yes; but the college chose the guide, we didn't, and her demeanor and candor seemed genuine (if disingenuous). More recently, we had a somewhat similar experience at Union College when we visited with my stepson, Andrew. A friend has observed that you are less likely to like a place if you visit when it rains. Maybe so, but that was not what turned us off about Trinity in Hartford. It is an undeniably first-rate college, but the guide and admissions counselor kept harping on how safe Hartford was. Right. A day later, after we visited Bates, I asked Andrew, "Did anyone here tell you how safe it is?" "No," he responded. "I guess they didn't have to because Lewiston is safe." Point made.

—EDWARD HERSHEY
PORTLAND, OREGON
🦅 3
🏛 CORNELL UNIVERSITY (2), COLORADO COLLEGE

I THINK YOU'LL NEVER REALLY UNDERSTAND why your kids pick one school over the other. My daughter went to visit her brother at Penn and said, "I need a dorm room bigger than a box; therefore I can't go to Penn." On one tour they pointed out the vegan restaurant and that just stuck in her head. She was like, "I'm not going here." It was one restaurant in such a lovely school, but that's what she focused on and that's how she made up her mind. You just never know what clicks with them.

—D.G.
SANTA MONICA, CALIFORNIA
👤 2
🏫 DREXEL UNIVERSITY; UNIVERSITY OF PENNSYLVANIA

• • • • • • • • •

WHEN YOU BEGIN VISITING COLLEGE CAMPUSES, make sure you don't schedule the same types of schools together on your first visit. If you are going to see several schools on your first visit, include a private and a public school and a large and a small campus or maybe a school in an urban area and one in a rural area. The first trip is really about ruling out kinds of schools not figuring out where you want to be.

—KATHIE
COOPERSBURG, PENNSYLVANIA
👤 2
🏫 PRINCIPIA COLLEGE; ROANOKE COLLEGE

WE VISITED 15 SCHOOLS, all in the Northeast. We took three or four road trips with him. He didn't want to do a lot of research on colleges until we were in the car and on our way, at which point he became very involved. It was really helpful for him to see the places, and some of it was just visceral reaction. He would look at the kids and say, "Uh, no, I don't see myself here."

—ANONYMOUS
BROOKLYN, NEW YORK
🎓 1
🏛 BROWN UNIVERSITY

• • • • • • • •

Our daughters got a feel for the culture and for the classroom facilities. And a visit introduced them to their peers. Those college student tour guides have tremendous impact on scared high school kids.

—ANN HAALAND
HIGHLAND, NEW YORK
🎓 2
🏛 GETTYSBURG COLLEGE; QUINNIPIAC UNIVERSITY

TOUR TIPS

Visiting colleges is a big test of the parent-child relationship. Your child is thinking: Is this a cool place where I can study what I want and have fun? You are thinking: How will this campus take care of my child? Will he be exposed to the right people, academics, and activities?

The biggest risk for the parent (and the greatest fear of the child) is that you will fatally embarrass him during the visit. Here are some tips to help you avoid the inevitable.

ASK INTELLIGENT QUESTIONS. Admissions officers should always be polite about any questions; it is their job to provide information. But don't step over the line and challenge the admissions officer, especially in a public presentation, on controversial issues. These questions may be posed in a private conversation.

ASK THE TOUR GUIDE ABOUT STUDENT LIFE and how the system works at the school. But don't ask questions based on your child. ("My son is really quiet and wants a room of his own.") Wait until after the tour to ask about availability of quiet dorms.

DON'T BE THE FAMILY SPOKESPERSON. If your child isn't asking questions, it's not a good sign. Make sure he asks some of the questions himself.

I'M NOT A BELIEVER IN VISITING COLLEGES before making a decision. I've found that the influencing factors that emerge from visits to schools are superficial. Students report on the weather, the coolness of their tour guide, the size of the dorm rooms, the age of the buildings. None of these aspects of a school determine the overall educational or social experience. I believe that the significant factors defining a school can be identified from talking with people and reading up on the school.

—BETH REINGOLD GLUCK
ATLANTA, GEORGIA
1

. . . .

WE ASKED A LOT OF QUESTIONS on the school tours. Most people ask very few. It became a family joke. I said to my husband, "These people on the tour with us are lucky. They're getting a lot more information than they would have without us." We each had our favorite questions to ask. My favorite was, "How late can you get food on campus?" My son is a night owl and I thought this might be an issue. Asking a lot of questions just gave us more information. They had to answer off the cuff. The more questions you ask, the more you get off the script.

—ANONYMOUS
BROOKLYN, NEW YORK
1
BROWN UNIVERSITY

WE WERE VISITING BOSTON and our son had no idea what school he was interested in attending. We said, "Why don't we just go to Harvard and look around?" He took one step onto the campus and he said, "I don't want to go here." We asked why, and he said, "It's too red." This was completely irrational, but he just said, "No, I'm not setting foot in that place. It is too red." There's a lot of intuition that goes into the kids' responses on these visits. There's a gut response on a primitive level. That one step on campus was enough for him.

—ANONYMOUS
ATLANTA, GEORGIA
🎓 1
🏛 BROWN UNIVERSITY

• • • • • • • •

IF YOU HAVE A YOUNGER CHILD, bring her along when you go on trips to colleges. We brought our daughter along on some of the trips when my son was looking, and because of this she had a head start. For example, she already knew that she wanted to be in a big city. My first child's list was all over the map, but since my daughter had seen some campuses already, her initial list was much more refined.

—R.K.
PHILADELPHIA, PENNSYLVANIA
🎓 1
🏛 UNIVERSITY OF PENNSYLVANIA

MY SON HAD TWO DIFFERENT EXPERIENCES on the trip. When we visited one of the schools, they were having their accepted-students weekend. They assign you to a student guide and there are all kinds of organized programs and activities going on. At another school we visited, he spent the morning there with a professor and the afternoon going to classes and visiting students. Ultimately he chose the school where he was able to spend time with the professor. The first was a hard-sell job and the second was low-key and much more about the school and what his daily experience there would be like.

—MARYANNE LAGUARDIA
SANTA MONICA, CALIFORNIA
🎓 2
🏛 BELOIT COLLEGE; UNIVERSITY OF ARIZONA

● ● ● ● ● ● ● ● ●

WE FOUND IT HELPFUL TO IDENTIFY and visit schools that span a wide range of possibilities just for perspective. We looked at small, medium, and large campuses. When our daughter started applying to schools later she could consider her target schools in comparison with the types of schools we actually visited.

—TOM
SAN FRANCISCO, CALIFORNIA
🎓 1
🏛 UNIVERSITY OF ARIZONA

MAKING A MATCH

Admissions officers use the term "match." What the heck does it mean? A good match is when the school meets most or all of the critical criteria your child needs in a school to be happy. What your child may perceive as most important items on the list:

1. Active social scene
2. Cool location
3. Great weather
4. Friends already there

What you should add to the list:

1. Right size both overall and in the classroom
2. Students and organizations both within and without your cultural/religious/ethnic group to both provide security and exposure to difference, in order to learn
3. Comfortable atmosphere—politically, academically

How do you help your child discover that this second list is necessary? Take some tours: this is the clearest way to assist, and you won't even have to try. Students will "feel" if a place seems right for them and will most likely direct themselves appropriately. Taking the official tour and getting the admissions spiel is just as important as the unofficial visits with friends; put together, they can give your child a strong sense of whether a college will be a match.

Focus: Narrowing the Choices

With admissions as competitive as they currently are, students will be wise to identify several schools at which they can see themselves. But after collecting all the colleges that seem to be interesting, you may end up with a frighteningly long list. How can you reduce that list of schools to a reasonable number?

Applying to a range of schools (i.e., big and small, suburban and urban) can be a good idea, but if your child knows he has a preference, let it guide your choices. It doesn't make sense to apply to every school in a certain area or category; many schools will not be a good fit, and the whole exercise will just be a waste of everyone's time and effort. It also does not make sense to apply to the top 25 schools as ranked by any one list—again, a waste of effort.

Research and advice are the secrets to creating the right school list. Read, read, and read some more about schools, on their Web sites and in college guides; talk to current students, alumni, and parents; listen to your high school guidance counselor; surf the Internet for opinions. (As always, consider the source when evaluating advice.) Tour some local schools on the weekends to get a sense of the college atmosphere—your child may not know something is important until he sees it—or a lack of it—on a campus.

While you want a thorough list of schools, make sure you and your child can explain what he loves about each school and provide rational reasons for applying for every one on his list. And no matter what you may think of a school, if he really cannot see himself on that campus, save your energy. There is no reason, with a well-researched and thoughtful list, to be applying to more than 10 schools.

ENCOURAGE YOUR CHILD NOT TO CHOOSE a school based on its reputation alone. There are several other factors that are important to consider, especially what type of school is the best match for your child based on his or her personality. Also, diversity, school size, and location etc., should be considered.

—T.W.
LITHONIA, GEORGIA
🎓 1
🏛 UNDECIDED

• • • • • • • • •

MY FIRST DAUGHTER KNEW she wanted to be an occupational therapist before she applied to college, so this helped narrow down our choices. She got into USC, which has one of the best programs in the country, so even though it's an expensive school, we had to send her there. Our other daughter wasn't so clear on what she wanted; she just knew she wanted to go to a large school in an urban setting. When she got into USC we didn't think it was necessary for her to go there, but how could we say no when her sister was already there? It would have been nice to save some money; our second daughter could have gone anywhere for a liberal arts education. My husband and I have always told them that if they work hard and get into where they want to go, then we would take care of the rest.

—J.H.
PASADENA, CALIFORNIA
🎓 2
🏛 UNIVERSITY OF SOUTHERN CALIFORNIA

MY SON AND I SPENT A SOBERING EVENING looking at acceptance scattergrams for various schools, which allow you to see how many students of a specific GPA and SAT score were accepted from a particular high school. This experience led him to remove some colleges that never accepted a student with his GPA, and led to a more realistic set of expectations. It's fine to have some reaches and apply to several schools, but applications are time-consuming, and those $75 fees really add up.

—RICHARD TYLER
REDMOND, WASHINGTON
🎓 1
🏛 NEW MEXICO INSTITUTE OF MINING & TECHNOLOGY

Don't let them choose a school that's so specialized that if they decide to change their major or course of study they'll be stuck.

—JENNIFER
CINCINNATI,
OHIO
🏛 MIAMI
UNIVERSITY OF
OHIO

• • • • • • • •

MY DAUGHTER KNEW THAT SHE WANTED to be a journalist, and she knew that she wanted to minor in photography. I called up people in the journalism profession to find out if certain schools could lead to better apprenticeships, internships, and job-placement opportunities. Just get on the phone and call up the public relations offices at companies that do the kind of business your child wants to get into. They were all happy to talk and help out.

—LAURIE BRESNICK
BEVERLY HILLS, CALIFORNIA
🎓 1
🏛 UNIVERSITY OF ARIZONA

MY HUSBAND AND I WENT TO HARVARD and thought our kids would follow in our footsteps. But our son decided that he only wanted to go to the University of Florida. We were the ones who had to adjust our expectations and decide we weren't going to be disappointed. This was to be the path he was going to take. If you have a child who is lukewarm about certain schools, don't push it. He can always go to grad school.

—ANONYMOUS
COOPER CITY, FLORIDA
🐘 3
University of Florida

• • • • • • • •

MY SON THOUGHT HE FOUND a school that sounded interesting. It was a good thing we visited the college; my son didn't like it all. I asked him to tell me what he disliked about the place and I wrote down his criteria. He said he wanted to go somewhere away from home but not too far. He decided on Pennsylvania. He applied to 11 schools. We visited about five of them, and he eliminated a few. After meeting with the head of the computer science department, he decided on Bloomsburg.

—ROBIN MALKI
WEST ORANGE, NEW JERSEY
🐘 1
Bloomsburg University

BEST SCHOOL, OR BEST TEAM?

MY SON PLAYS BASKETBALL, and when athletics enters the decision-making process, you add a whole extra element that makes your decision harder. First, you have to figure out how good your child is and what division and level he or she can play at. Sometimes the lower-division schools are higher on an academic scale and may not be a good fit. You will not be doing your child a favor if you get them into a good school as a player while at the same time one that is too academically advanced for them, because they will never graduate. You have to be realistic and ask yourself if your decision is being ego-driven or if you want your kid to feel good about school. It's so hard for them to play sports because the teams practice at least five days a week for many hours. Being an athlete is like having a full time job while going to school, and that, combined with living away from home for the first time, is a tough experience.

—ANONYMOUS
LOS ANGELES, CALIFORNIA
♟ 2
🏛 CALIFORNIA STATE UNIVERSITY, NORTHRIDGE;
SANTA MONICA CITY COLLEGE

TRUST A COLLEGE COACH like you would a Hollywood agent—don't trust him at all. My daughter was on the track team in high school and her times were good enough for her to go to a Division III school. It was very flattering for our daughter, to get calls from coaches, but these coaches are salesmen and they were just buttering her up to get her to choose their school. She really liked one of the coaches and had so many phone conversations with him that she started considering him a friend. He called one day and I had to tell him that she chose another school to attend. After that, he never called again. It hurt her feelings. I had to explain to her that the coach's job is simply to recruit; once they know you aren't interested, they move on to the next potential student.

—C.T.
SANTA MONICA, CALIFORNIA
♟ 2
SIMMONS COLLEGE; CORNELL UNIVERSITY

MY DAUGHTER AND I EACH MADE A CHART with different criteria on it and used that to organize the application process and the financial aid offers. Talk to your kid in a calm manner about how you feel and how they feel. Ultimately it has to be their choice. My daughter thought she really wanted to go to a school I wasn't too crazy about and I supported her in her choice, but made sure she got a taste of other schools too, and she changed her mind.

—KATHLEEN RIDER
HYDE PARK, NEW YORK
🎓 4
🏫 STATE UNIVERSITY OF NEW YORK (2); FORDHAM UNIVERSITY; QUINNIPIAC UNIVERSITY

* * * * * * * * *

OUR SON WAS VERY FOCUSED on mathematics or engineering as his major. But a few of the schools he liked did not offer a wide variety of options should he decide that neither of those areas appealed to him, or if he was denied acceptance into the programs. Bringing that detail to his attention definitely drove our son to take another look at the schools, and those that didn't have many other options for him were weeded out, taking his list from seven schools to three.

—ANONYMOUS
KENT, WASHINGTON
🎓 2
🏫 WASHINGTON STATE UNIVERSITY; UNIVERSITY OF WASHINGTON

WHEN YOU APPLY TO ELITE SCHOOLS, even if you are overqualified, you might not get in. My son knew at the age of six that he wanted to learn about epidemiology and infectious diseases. We thought that with this kind of passion, combined with his scores and grades, he would definitely get into Yale as an early-decision candidate. Well, he didn't, and at that point he had to come up with other options. He got into six of eleven schools he applied to. Still, some of the schools that accepted him were a lot harder to get into than some of the ones that rejected him. You just don't know.

—BERURAH RUNYON
DERBY, KANSAS
🎓 1
🏛 DUKE UNIVERSITY

• • • • • • • •

MY DAUGHTER WAS TRULY STRETCHED for time when we started to contact schools, so I helped her put together a student-athlete profile and sent this out to numerous track coaches. Once she had some interest from coaches at other schools, it broadened her thinking and really made her consider what would be the best situation for her.

—ANONYMOUS
HIGHLANDS RANCH, COLORADO
🎓 1
🏛 UNDECIDED

You've got to let the kids make their own decision, unless it is really harmful. It's the first thing they really own.

—*ANONYMOUS
BROOKLYN,
NEW YORK*
🏛 *BROWN
UNIVERSITY*

ORGANIZATION TIPS

With so many schools to research and learn about, you and your child need to get organized. Here are some field-tested tips:

- Have your child set up a new e-mail account for all college correspondence, using a respectable, mature, account name.

- Create folders for each school to which your child will definitely be applying. Include all brochures, and make a list on the front of the folder of all the requirements, the deadlines, and the essay questions.

- See where essay topics overlap and try to minimize essay writing. (If essays do not fit other schools, though, do not reuse them. It is obvious and shows laziness or a lack of interest by refusing to follow directions).

- Post a wall calendar and mark all deadlines. Plan backwards and set interim deadlines to help reach the big ones.

MY SON ALWAYS KNEW that he wanted to major in computer science and also he wanted to go to a big school with a lot of school spirit. I got a list of schools that fit his criteria, and I spent several days researching online. I looked up college rankings from *U.S. News & World Report* to see which schools were highest academically, and then I had to ask my husband about school spirit, since I know nothing about sports. I found one school that was in the top five for computer science that had everything else my son was looking for, and that's where he goes. He couldn't be happier.

—L.R.
SCOTTSDALE, ARIZONA
🎓 1
🏛 UNIVERSITY OF CALIFORNIA, BERKELEY

• • • • • • • •

AS A PARENT YOU WANT THE BEST FOR THEM. This is a teaching moment for you; it's a way to help your kids make big decisions, so in the future when you aren't there for them they will be able to make these tough choices on their own.

—PETER
SEATTLE, WASHINGTON
🎓 1
🏛 SWARTHMORE COLLEGE

HELP YOUR CHILDREN RESEARCH SCHOOLS and have them give you very specific reasons why they want to go. My daughter has always been pretty independent, so when she said she wanted to do it on her own, I trusted that she knew what she was talking about. She ended up applying to 15 schools, got accepted to most of them, chose one of them and hated it. Since then she's transferred twice and is still unhappy. I didn't realize until after the fact that she was randomly choosing colleges based on where her friends were going. If I could do it all over again, I would sit down with her and make her write down three reasons for choosing each school. And if she didn't have three reasons, I would discourage her from applying.

—G.V.
HOUSTON, TEXAS
2
UNIVERSITY OF TEXAS, AUSTIN;
UNIVERSITY OF MICHIGAN

There are so many wonderful schools out there; keep an open mind.

—T.S.
LOS ANGELES,
CALIFORNIA
DUKE
UNIVERSITY

• • • • • • • •

IF THERE IS ANYTHING YOUR CHILD is interested in, use it to help narrow down the choices. My first daughter plays field hockey and she knew that she wanted to play at a Division III school. Also, she was a very good student, so she focused on small, high-ranking liberal arts schools that offered varsity field hockey. Using those criteria, a lot of schools were immediately eliminated.

—LUCY RUMACK
BROOKLYN, NEW YORK
1
SWARTHMORE COLLEGE

WHEN I WAS YOUNG we had Christmas break and spring break. Now they have all of these breaks that I don't even think existed. They come home for all of the holidays and any journey longer than ten hours gets to be a drag for them.

—ANONYMOUS
NORTH POTOMAC, MARYLAND
2
BRANDEIS UNIVERSITY; CORNELL UNIVERSITY

* * * * * * * * *

MY DAUGHTER WAS CHOOSING between two state schools, one rated higher than the other. She was pretty sure she wanted to go to the higher ranked school, but before making her final decision, she went to visit both and stayed with freshmen in the dorms. It was a really good way for her to get a true experience of what life on both campuses was like.

—KAREN
SCOTTSDALE, ARIZONA
1
UNIVERSITY OF ARIZONA

* * * * * * * * *

OUR SCHOOL ADVISED PARENTS to apply to the state system as an automatic safety. My daughter refused, saying, "I won't go there, so why waste an application?" She didn't, and she was right.

—N.
NEW YORK, NEW YORK
1
CARLETON COLLEGE

MOTHER, FATHER AND THE ALMA MATER

"Wow, I want to go back to college" is a comment admissions officers frequently hear when talking to parents of visiting high school students. They hear it most often when parents are visiting their own alma maters.

Visits stir up your old college memories, especially if you are touring your own college. As nostalgia starts to flow, be careful that your memories of the past do not cloud the future. Your school was clearly your match—you loved it and you thrived—but your child is not you, and the school is not the same place 30 years later. Encourage your child to consider your alma mater, but do not be wounded if it is not her match.

As a legacy applicant, your child *might* get a boost in the admissions process, but be sure to research each school's policy. At some schools, your child could get a big boost. At others, it is only influential in the decision if your child is already 98-percent admissible on her own. If a legacy applicant is well below the admissions standard, you would be a kinder parent not to encourage that application, as many schools will not stretch too far to admit alumni-related students.

It bears repeating: your child's success depends on being at a school where she can thrive. This means she is spiritually comfortable, feels academically confident, and can play a role in campus life. Encouraging applications to schools where children are not within the statistical parameters can be hurtful. You can harm your child by encouraging applications to too many "reach" schools. The school's name on your bumper sticker may make *you* happy, but this is not about you. If your child will be overwhelmed in class, or by people too unlike him, or in an uncomfortable location, your dreams of high achievement will be dashed. With the right fit, the grades will come, and so will the launching pad for life.

BEFORE YOU APPLY TO OUT-OF-TOWN COLLEGES, check the flight schedule. My daughter goes to school in New Orleans, we live in Phoenix, and there is one airline with one nonstop flight each day. Sometimes my daughter comes home for just a few days and has to spend two full days flying because she can't get the nonstop flight.

—J.M.
SCOTTSDALE, ARIZONA
1
LOYOLA UNIVERSITY, NEW ORLEANS

• • • • • • • •

IF YOU HAVE A KID who has no idea where she wants to go, figure out what she might want to do once she graduates, and look for schools with programs in that particular subject. My oldest could not come up with her own list, but I thought she would do well in either business or engineering. At first she said, "Mom, engineering is so hard." I replied that a philosophy major might say engineering is hard, but if you had a choice to write a paper or solve a math problem, which one would you choose? Of course, she said the math problem. At that point I started looking for schools that had accreditation for engineering and schools that had accredited business schools. She ended up going to Lehigh in their integrated business and engineering program.

—J.M.
ARLINGTON, VIRGINIA
2
LEHIGH UNIVERSITY; ELON UNIVERSITY

WE NARROWED OUR CHOICES DOWN to location: in case of emergency, I wanted to be able to get to my daughters by automobile. When they started to look at schools, I told them that they couldn't go any farther than a 10-hour drive from home. Not everyone should set limits like I do, but this is my comfort zone.

—ANONYMOUS
NORTH POTOMAC, MARYLAND
♟ 2
🏛 BRANDEIS UNIVERSITY; CORNELL UNIVERSITY

* * * * * * * *

Whatever isn't immoral, illegal, or permanent is their choice. Save your battles.

—BETTY JEAN NEAL
TOPEKA, KANSAS

* * * * * * * *

MAKE SURE YOUR KIDS APPLY to a couple of schools that are within at least three hours driving distance. I know a lot of students who said that they wanted to get away and go really far from home when they were looking at colleges. But when push came to shove in April, they really didn't want to be so far from home.

—V.A.
AUSTIN, TEXAS
♟ 2
🏛 RICE UNIVERSITY; UNIVERSITY OF TEXAS, AUSTIN

DON'T AUTOMATICALLY THROW AWAY those pamphlets that come in the mail! During my son's junior year in high school, he began getting solicitations from dozens of colleges, all of which promptly went into the trash can, since he was determined to go to a Missouri state school. By sheer chance, my partner intercepted a postcard from California State University in Monterey Bay—2,000 miles and two time zones away from home. When she showed it to my son, he glanced at it and tossed it aside. But two months later, he announced that he'd applied on his own because he'd wanted to go to California his "whole life." He was accepted, and we held our breath as he set out for school, not knowing a soul there. Within a few weeks, he'd made tons of friends, found a part-time job and had traveled extensively up and down the coast—he absolutely loves it!

> —N.L.
> ST. LOUIS, MISSOURI
> 🎓 2
> 🏛 TRUMAN STATE UNIVERSITY;
> CALIFORNIA STATE UNIVERSITY, MONTEREY BAY

• • • • • • • •

IF YOUR CHILD IS INTERESTED in a certain field it's important to choose the most prestigious school. A big-name university helps open doors; it can lead to important connections throughout a person's entire career and life.

> —MARY
> TIBURON, CALIFORNIA
> 🎓 2
> 🏛 COLORADO UNIVERSITY, BOULDER;
> CLAREMONT MCKENNA COLLEGE

Getting Help: School Resources & Private Counselors

As complicated as the college admissions process can become, one thing you can be sure of is that everyone is confused; you are not alone. You and your child will most likely have access to a guidance counselor at your child's high school who can help direct your child to appropriate schools for him. Your high school counselor is a partner in this process.

Try to figure out how to maximize the counselor-student-parent relationship as it works in your high school. Depending on his knowledge and availability, a school's college counselor can be a great asset to you in the process. However, in many schools across the country there are simply not enough counselors to take care of the students in a personal way. If you are unable to get the assistance you need from the high school, you should consider help from an independent college counselor.

In some parts of the country, independent counselors seem almost as required as test preparation courses. A whole industry has sprung up in the last few years to address—and to prey on—the fear parents have that they will make a mistake. Depending on your community, you may get caught up in this frenzy for assistance.

Independent counselors can be wonderful resources and guides in the admissions process, providing information and emotional support for you and your child. They can motivate the child in ways a parent cannot. But you may be in for a hefty investment, and without proper research, you might find yourselves in an unhelpful relationship. Assess your needs well before committing to this relationship.

How do you know how much extra help you need? Truly, with some time and research savvy, most students and parents can figure out the process to a reasonable degree. Families without this ability—often with children who will be the first generation heading to college—will be given the benefit of the doubt in their applications if something may not be done "perfectly." Assess your available time and your abilities to be able to make the best decision for your child and your family.

HIRE A COLLEGE CONSULTANT to lift the burden from your shoulders. Ours created an engine of activity for our youngest daughter, which made the year leading up to applications completely stress-free in comparison to the year before with our middle daughter. Our youngest arrived on the first day of her senior year with all of her common applications submitted, having completed the winnowing of schools that mapped to her interests, threshold for distance from home, and our budget.

—LORING EDMONDS
MILLIS, MASSACHUSETTS
♟ 2
ARIZONA STATE UNIVERSITY; FRAMINGHAM STATE UNIVERSITY

• • • • • • • • •

DON'T ASSUME THE COUNSELORS have done their job—check up on them! Many weeks after applying, my son called a prospective college to see when he would be getting an answer. They told him they'd never received his grades! Another phone call to the counselor's office revealed they had dropped the ball, but, thankfully, there was still enough time to get his grades out before the deadline.

—N.L.
ST. LOUIS, MISSOURI
♟ 2
TRUMAN STATE UNIVERSITY;
CALIFORNIA STATE UNIVERSITY, MONTEREY BAY

I AM FROM MINNESOTA, and for people in Minnesota getting "hired help" means someone helps you with your storm windows in the winter. I guess because I'm from Minnesota I have this do-it-yourself mentality. My daughter had good grades and a lot of extracurricular activities, and I just didn't think her acceptance relied on whether or not I hired someone to help her. She did get into her first-choice school, and I think the advice that worked best was telling her to really try to be her true self.

—ANONYMOUS
LOS ANGELES, CALIFORNIA
🎓 1
🏛 UNIVERSITY OF CALIFORNIA, SANTA BARBARA

• • • • • • • • •

COLLEGE COUNSELORS ARE BASICALLY USELESS. They had a list prepared before our visit, which, to my mind must have been schools where their friends worked or gave them a kickback. They were "in the box" schools, and I think my kids did a better job finding schools in *Barron's Guide to Colleges.* The counselors didn't have too many interesting suggestions for us.

—MIRIAM SILVERMAN
ELKINS PARK, PENNSYLVANIA
🎓 2
🏛 SYRACUSE UNIVERSITY; UNIVERSITY OF MARYLAND

THE GUIDANCE COUNSELOR AT OUR HIGH SCHOOL had my daughter and her three friends make up "college stress charts" that they put on his office wall. The bottom axis was time, with a bunch of dates. Then each kid had numbers on the vertical axis. One of her friends went from 0 to a million! Every few weeks they would go in and put a dot for the date and the level of stress they were experiencing.

—SUSAN
NEW ENGLAND
1
BROWN UNIVERSITY

• • • • • • • • •

The guidance counselor at my son's school is not very helpful. There are 1,800 kids in his class, so you don't get much individual attention. I was basically his guidance counselor. Sometimes you have to take charge.

—JORDAN CASELL
STAFFORD, VIRGINIA
1
UNDECIDED

LONG-HAUL COUNSELING

We were the overzealous, West Los Angeles parents when it came to getting our first child into college. We started with a private counselor in the ninth grade because our son went to public school. We signed up for the four-year package; in retrospect, that was a little too much. At the time we didn't want to feel that we missed anything. Included in the package was a meeting in the beginning to discuss high school class load and review of our son's schedule to make sure he was taking the most competitive classes the school had to offer. That was pretty much all the counselor was good for in ninth and tenth grade. Junior year, the counselor helped us pick schools and decide where to visit. During senior year our counselor was heavily involved in editing the essays. My second child just started college this year and we waited until spring semester of her sophomore year to sign up with a counselor.

—D.G.
SANTA MONICA, CALIFORNIA
2
DREXEL UNIVERSITY; UNIVERSITY OF PENNSYLVANIA

MY HUSBAND AND I DIDN'T GO to college so we were pretty lost during the whole process. We relied heavily on our daughter's academic advisor for everything. Our daughter's advisor helped her choose two reach schools, two schools that she would most likely get into, and two safety schools. She got into one of her reaches, so sometimes I think her counselor didn't advise her to reach high enough. If I had done my own research I might have advised her otherwise.

—NANCY
LAS VEGAS, NEVADA
1
DUKE UNIVERSITY

• • • • • • • •

I AM A SINGLE MOTHER and I work full time, so even though I tried to stay ahead and on top of things for my daughter, I felt like I was always one step behind. The task seemed overwhelming for a teenager, so I hired a private counselor. It was a stretch financially, but it was worth every penny. My daughter got into her first-choice school, and I am almost certain that without the help it would never have happened.

—TRACY
CHICAGO, ILLINOIS
1
WASHINGTON UNIVERSITY

The best counselors served as guideposts and objective listeners, and helped suggest appropriate timeline strategies.

—SHARON
PHILADELPHIA, PENNSYLVANIA
WESLEYAN UNIVERSITY;
WASHINGTON &
LEE UNIVERSITY

I LOOKED AT WHAT OTHER PARENTS WERE DOING. When I saw that other parents were hiring private college counselors I questioned my initial decision to forgo one. We finally hired someone midway through senior year, and it really helped. I only wish we had hired someone sooner. My daughter really wanted to go to Yale; she didn't get accepted, and I think if we'd hired a counselor earlier on, she might have gotten in.

—T.S.
LOS ANGELES, CALIFORNIA
🎓 1
🏛 DUKE UNIVERSITY

• • • • • • • •

ONE THING COLLEGE COUNSELORS can help with is preparation for admissions interviews. My son's counselor did a sort of mock interview with him, asking him the questions that are typically asked in real interviews, and helping him prepare questions to ask the admissions officers. It was only a half-hour session, but it really helped him know what to expect.

—CAMILLE
CINCINNATI, OHIO
🎓 1
🏛 UNIVERSITY OF KENTUCKY

ASSISTANTS, NOT MAGICIANS

A private consultant can be immensely helpful to both your child and you: He may know schools well and be able to suggest good matches, especially those that could be overlooked; he can take some of the planning and research off of your hands; he can support you all emotionally through the roller-coaster process. But there are limits to his powers. For one thing, he cannot advocate for your child in any way and he has no power with college admissions offices. Your child should be communicating directly with the schools, and the only other acceptable advocate (aside from you) is his high school guidance counselor, who can call the college on his behalf.

Private college counseling is cottage industry, with consultants of varying skills and experience cropping up in every corner. There are some who know nothing and give bad information. Good consultants attend professional conferences, belong to professional admissions organizations, visit campuses, push your child to find his best match by suggesting an appropriate list, and help your child gain admission on his merits, without gimmicks. They are out there; choose wisely.

QUESTIONS TO ASK WHEN LOOKING FOR A PRIVATE COUNSELOR

The key to finding a good private counselor is assessing his experience in the admissions field. A good counselor sees his role as a professional—he is an expert who does this as a profession, versus a way to make money from a topical issue. Ask for recommendations, check out the established places in your area, then answer the following questions:

- How many years has the counselor been in this profession?

- Has he worked on college admissions staffs before?

- Has he been a high school guidance counselor?

- Do you trust his writing ability?

- Does he have advanced degrees in counseling or education?

- Does he participate in NACAC, the professional organization?

- Does he regularly take college tours to keep current?

- Is his personality and work style a fit with your child and with you?

AT MY SON'S SCHOOL, each high school counselor is responsible for about 150 students. That is way too many students for each child to get the individualized attention and college plan that they need.

—M.H.
ELLENWOOD, GEORGIA
🎓 1
🏫 LANDER UNIVERSITY

• • • • • • • •

BE REALISTIC WITH YOUR EXPECTATIONS for your child's high school college counselor. My daughter's school had four counselors working for about 200 college applicants, and there was only so much they could do. If the student initiated a question, the counselor would help, but that was about as far as it went.

—LESLIE KUHLMAN
CINCINNATI, OHIO
🎓 1
🏫 FRANCISCAN UNIVERSITY OF STEUBENVILLE

• • • • • • • •

IF YOUR CHILD IS RIGHT in the middle academically, I don't think there is a reason to pay a high-priced advisor to help with the application process. My daughter has good grades and scores, but we knew there was no way she would get into an Ivy League school. We didn't need someone with a relationship with an Ivy school, because we knew we couldn't get there.

—LAURIE BRESNICK
BEVERLY HILLS, CALIFORNIA
🎓 1
🏫 UNIVERSITY OF ARIZONA

THE MAIN THING WE HAD PROBLEMS WITH in the college process was getting extended time for the SAT and ACT. To go to the College Board and ask for that extra time is a huge ordeal, because you have to provide all this documentation and it can get "lost." My son's guidance counselor was by my side the whole time, helping in any way she could.

—MONA GLOVER
CINCINNATI, OHIO
🎓 1
🏛 KENYON COLLEGE

. . . .

AFTER GOING THROUGH THE COLLEGE application process four times in six years, the best advice I can give is not to get overinvolved or worried. It's the guidance counselor's job to help your child apply and get accepted. Step back and enjoy those junior and senior years. Enjoy your children, because they will soon be gone and your job as parents will be over.

—DEE A. MARTIN
MADEIRA, OHIO
🎓 4
🏛 UNIVERSITY OF DAYTON; WITTENBERG UNIVERSITY; BOSTON UNIVERSITY; SAINT LOUIS UNIVERSITY

Endurance: The Application Process

The chips are finally hitting the table—it is time to fill out the applications and complete all the requirements. This phase of the process will take over your child's life (and yours), but with some planning, you can minimize the highest stress factor: procrastination. Worse than the stress on you is that colleges can clearly see the results of procrastination, when an application is thrown together sloppily at the last minute. So, help your child pace himself to avoid this potentially application-sabotaging act.

The best way to survive the physical process is by organization. Assess the applications' needs and make lists and timetables with your child to help him accomplish them. There are a few time savers—for example, the Common Application. While partially responsible for some of the new "overapplication"—or less-thoughtful-application—frenzy these days, the Common Application will be a significant time-saver if your child is applying to multiple schools that accept it. This means he fills out the Common App once, online; sends it to all the schools that accept it; and saves the time of filling out all of his infor-mation and activities for each of the schools. Additionally, if schools do not require supplemental essays, he will only have to write one—strong!— essay for the Common App. Avert another stress-inducer: help him plan how to accomplish the things he may forget, such as asking teachers for recommendations in plenty of time.

Motivation to fill out all the applications may really start to flag after the novelty of the process wears off. In the beginning, it may seem romantic to be filling out all the forms—but then reality hits: there are several more schools waiting in line. Prepare to provide some psychological support. And, you may be able to motivate him to plug away by offering incentives. What better time could there be to reward extra effort on your child's part?

HELP YOUR KIDS FIND THEIR STRONG SUIT. My daughter was freaking out over the essay portion, insisting that she was not a good writer. We got into some knockdown fights. The deadline was approaching and she was procrastinating. But I started talking to her about the creative process of the essay. I know my daughter, and I knew she was creative. Soon she came up with some great essay ideas. For one, she interviewed herself for a fictitious magazine called *Want To Be Weekly*. One of her student projects was a film that won a "Top 12 in the Nation" award for high school student films. She interviewed herself about the film, the process of making it and how it came about.

—TERRY
IRVINE, CALIFORNIA
🎓 1
🏛 MOUNT HOLYOKE COLLEGE

• • • • • • • •

WE SAT DOWN AT OUR KITCHEN COUNTER, side by side, with two laptops. She did one application while I did another. We set up a notebook with a tab for each college and then we filled in information about each, made a checklist for what we had sent in and when, and noted each school's deadlines. It has been a good time for us; very much a bonding time. High school graduation is a sad time, so getting excited about the possibilities of college helps.

—B.D.
MCDONOUGH, GEORGIA
🎓 1
🏛 DUKE UNIVERSITY

IT'S REALLY IMPORTANT TO KNOW your kid's strengths and weaknesses. My son can just sit down and ace standardized tests, but trying to get him to write essays is like pulling teeth. So, I had to get on him about that. Plus, he's more of a geek type, so it's harder for him to sell himself in interviews. My daughter, on the other hand, is great in interviews, but it is really difficult for her to study for the SATs; I had to push her to take an SAT prep course. It's important to understand who they are as people, so you can tailor the way you help them prepare.

—JORDAN CASELL
STAFFORD, VIRGINIA
🎓 1
🏛 UNDECIDED

• • • • • • • •

Parents should help their kids as much as the child needs or asks for. If the child thinks he can do it by himself, great. If he asks for help, be happy that he asked!

—URSULA ARMSTRONG
MARKESAN, WISCONSIN
🎓 1
🏛 STEVENS POINT UNIVERSITY

I GOT TOO WORKED UP about my daughter completing her applications before she came back from summer break. She went to Florida on vacation, and when I asked about her applications, she told me over the phone that she was not coming back and was not going to college. Once I calmed down, she calmed down. As the parent, you have the responsibility of setting the tone for patience, levelheaded thinking and staying focused on the big stuff. Let them see that you are actually listening to them by asking for their suggestions and not acting like you
are the pro.

—R.F.
ATLANTA, GEORGIA
1
UNIVERSITY OF PENNSYLVANIA

• • • • • • • •

HAVE YOUR CHILD COMPLETE the college essays early. Writing an essay doesn't sound that difficult, but once they sit down to do it they realize what a challenge it is. My daughter turned in her essay to her first-choice school about three weeks before it was due. Her friends were actually writing their essays three hours before they were due! And some of them missed the deadline because the schools' computers were jammed with too much traffic from everyone else trying to submit their essays.

—ANONYMOUS
LOS ANGELES, CALIFORNIA
1
UNIVERSITY OF CALIFORNIA, SANTA BARBARA

ABOUT THOSE ESSAYS

ENGLISH TEACHERS CAN BE A GREAT RESOURCE for those college essays. The first part of the year my son's teacher helped him with the planning and writing of the essays, and then once he had finished she took the time to look them over and tweak them a bit. Just having someone read them who knew a little more about what admissions officers were looking for was really helpful for him.

—DONNA
CINCINNATI, OHIO
♉ 2
🏛 MIAMI UNIVERSITY (2)

• • • • • • • •

MY DAUGHTER WANTED TO WRITE about her story of overcoming depression and it was really hard to convince her otherwise. I took her to several professional college counselors and they all advised her that it could blacklist her from getting in. We were told that admissions committees shy away from students with mental disabilities because the schools want to protect themselves from lawsuits.

—ANONYMOUS
LOS ANGELES, CALIFORNIA
♉ 2
🏛 UNIVERSITY OF CALIFORNIA, LOS ANGELES;
UNIVERSITY OF CALIFORNIA, BERKELEY

I LET MY DAUGHTER BE RESPONSIBLE for her own essays. I basically gave her some tips before she started. Like, stick to her topic, be herself, and try to write in a conversational tone. I also advised her to read it out loud to herself. She said that piece of advice helped the most in terms of catching errors.

—MELISSA
LOS ANGELES, CALIFORNIA
🏆 1
🏛 UNIVERSITY OF CALIFORNIA, SAN DIEGO

• • • • • • • • •

ADVISE YOUR KIDS TO KEEP THEIR ESSAYS to one page. If someone with ten years of work experience can fit their résumé on one page, then a 17-year-old kid should be able to edit his essay down to a page. The admissions officers are really busy and have so many applications to read. You don't want them to lose interest. One school we went to explained it really well: they said it's an application, not a dissertation.

—JANE
SCOTTSDALE, ARIZONA
🏆 1
🏛 UNIVERSITY OF MIAMI

WHEN IT CAME TIME TO WRITE her first college essay, my daughter went upstairs and came down just a few hours later with her idea of a finished product. She handed me this boring paper; I couldn't believe what I was reading. I said, "If this is the amount of time and energy you want to put into this, then that's fine, but you better revamp your list of schools; you are applying to a lot of the Ivies and some highly selective schools." When you have kids who always do well in school; when all of their teachers love them, they believe that the admissions officers are going to love them just as much. Somehow my daughter thought she could just check off all of the boxes on her application and get in. That's not good enough.

—L.L.
GLOBAL NOMAD
2
HARVARD UNIVERSITY; BROWN UNIVERSITY

• • • • • • • •

YOU WANT TO MAKE SURE YOUR CHILD'S ESSAY reflects him, and not something he thinks the admissions folks want to hear. I imagine that admissions officers can pick up on the prepackaged essays that are written by someone else, so make sure your kid gets his personality to show through, somewhere.

—PETER
SEATTLE, WASHINGTON
1
SWARTHMORE COLLEGE

I ADVISED MY CHILDREN to apply early decision: 1) It afforded a better chance of getting in (regardless of what the colleges claimed). 2) It let the student know where he or she stood early enough to focus on good alternatives if necessary. 3) If the student did get in, it made for a gloriously pressure-free spring.

> —EDWARD HERSHEY
> PORTLAND, OREGON
> 👕 3
> 🏫 CORNELL UNIVERSITY (2), COLORADO COLLEGE

• • • • • • • •

IF YOUR CHILD WANTS TO GO TO COLLEGE it's important to have her do most of the grunt work while applying. After all, you won't be sitting in class holding her hand, so why help her up to the high-dive platform when she'll be left to dive in by herself?

> —ANNETTE
> GERMANTOWN, MARYLAND
> 👕 2
> 🏫 JAMES MADISON UNIVERSITY;
> UNIVERSITY OF MARYLAND, COLLEGE PARK

• • • • • • • •

REGARDLESS OF THE DEADLINE, get your applications in by the first of November; don't wait until the last minute. I understand that some people have to hold off because of finances, but if money isn't an issue, get it done early and enjoy the holidays.

> —ANONYMOUS
> DEERFIELD, ILLINOIS
> 👕 1
> 🏫 VANDERBILT UNIVERSITY

INSIDE THE INTERVIEW

MY DAUGHTER INTERVIEWED AT SEVERAL SCHOOLS and each time the interviewer brought up politics. Fortunately, my daughter is caught up on current events and has strong opinions. When she came to me after the first time she was politically challenged in her interview, I advised her not to back down and to verbalize her opinion along with strong supporting statements. Although I would never suggest that the student start up a conversation on politics, I would definitely engage if asked. Tell your kids not to agree with the interviewer if it isn't what they truly believe. These people are asking these questions for a reason. I think they want to see if you have an opinion, if you know what's going on in the world, if you have passion, and if you can support your position.

—ANONYMOUS
PHILADELPHIA, PENNSYLVANIA
1
SMITH COLLEGE

· · · · · · · ·

ONE ALUMNI INTERVIEWER REALLY TOOK A LIKING to my daughter. He sent *her* a thank-you note!

—N
NEW YORK, NEW YORK
1
CARLETON COLLEGE

I'M AN ALUMNI INTERVIEWER and some of my better interviews involved kids with interests in topics they could intellectually discuss. I remember one kid who was doing research on alternative energy and new fuel options for automobiles. She was very articulate on the subject and it was a refreshing change. The opposite case was when a student said he was really interested in constitutions. He brought up the European Union constitution and talked about how it was coming up for a vote, but he had no ideas or knowledge about its failures in some other countries. He oversold his interest about it. The best way to come across is to have a genuine interest in something and be informed about it. Trying to search the Internet for knowledge the day or week before the interview probably isn't going to work.

—PETER
SEATTLE, WASHINGTON
1
SWARTHMORE COLLEGE

KEEPING TRACK OF ALL THE INFORMATION is a big job. Sometimes it's better to have one parent spearhead the effort. Throughout grade school I was the parent involved with my kids' schoolwork. But truthfully, my husband is more organized, so he got the job of the college application process. He was the one to drive them to visit schools and even helped them move in. Then I took over. I think it was a good way to divide things.

—MARY
TIBURON, CALIFORNIA
2
COLORADO UNIVERSITY, BOULDER;
CLAREMONT MCKENNA COLLEGE

. . . .

Applying to college almost begs for managerial skills. Kids don't have the perspective of parents. It's good and helpful for parents to offer their perspective, given how competitive the whole process is.

—KAREN BARCHAS
TRUCKEE, CALIFORNIA
1
UNIVERSITY OF CALIFORNIA, BERKELEY

KEEP FOLLOWING UP

My daughter was wait-listed at one of the schools she applied to and then rejected. The college admissions office said they never received her high school transcript, but the high school gave us proof that they sent it. My daughter got copies of everything, walked into the college's admissions office and handed everything over in person. We still had to wait two weeks and it was time to say yes or no to the other schools. They ultimately accepted her, but it was too little too late. The lesson we learned from all of this is how important it is to follow up. Some colleges offer an online checklist where you can see what they received and what they are still waiting for. Keep following up until you get a confirmation that everything has been received.

—D.G.
SANTA MONICA, CALIFORNIA
♟ 2
🏛 DREXEL UNIVERSITY; UNIVERSITY OF PENNSYLVANIA

OUR SON DID MOST OF HIS APPLICATIONS ONLINE. He sent them in at 10 p.m. on the night of the deadline, New Year's Eve. He went down to the wire. We were ready to strangle him, and meanwhile he pushed that button to send off his applications and went out for New Year's Eve. There is no easy way to encourage them. Sometimes you just have to let them fail in order to learn. Our son is that kind of kid. But it stressed out the whole family.

—ANONYMOUS
BROOKLYN, NEW YORK
🏺 1
🏛 BROWN UNIVERSITY

* * * * * * * * *

THE SCHOOLS SAY THEY CAN TELL real passion from contrived passion. My daughter had been dancing her whole life, but stopped in order to focus on her grades. That summer we took a vacation in Africa and she wrote her essay about that experience. The essay was fine, but I couldn't feel the passion. Then she wrote a really short essay about dancing that she titled, "The Girl With the Ugly Feet." It was beautiful; you could just feel the passion.

—D.G.
SANTA MONICA, CALIFORNIA
🏺 2
🏛 DREXEL UNIVERSITY; UNIVERSITY OF PENNSYLVANIA

Papers get lost in the mail. When you send anything to a college, make copies first and send everything "Return Receipt Requested."

—ANONYMOUS
NORTH POTOMAC, MARYLAND
🏛 BRANDEIS UNIVERSITY; CORNELL UNIVERSITY

THE PERSONAL TOUCH

IF YOU WANT TO TIP THE SCALES, visit the dean of the department your child is trying to get into. My son had a specific skill, which was music. Once my son chose his two top schools, I called the music department in both of those schools, spoke to the dean and said we would be in the neighborhood and would like to stop by and say hello. Just be proactive and call the department yourself. This way, your child is no longer just a faceless application; you actually get to meet the person who ultimately will decide if your kid gets accepted.

> —ANONYMOUS
> BEVERLY HILLS, CALIFORNIA
> 🎓 1
> 🏛 NORTHEASTERN UNIVERSITY

* * * * * * * * *

MY SON WENT TO INFORMATION SESSIONS for all of the schools he applied to. Sometimes he was the only one there, so he was able to spend time talking with the person who might ultimately decide his fate. He was also able to get personal e-mail addresses at these events; and after each one, he followed up with an e-mail or a letter thanking the person for meeting him.

> —R.K.
> PHILADELPHIA, PENNSYLVANIA
> 🎓 1
> 🏛 UNIVERSITY OF PENNSYLVANIA

EARLY DECISION IS RIGHT IF ...

- Your child has identified a true front-runner school, at which he can see himself above all others, by visiting in person;

- You can afford the cost (either fully or with estimated aid);

- There are no doubts about the fit between your child and the school—you are committing to it;

- Your child has time to complete all testing in advance and is confident that his grades have so far been a good representation of his ability.

BEFORE MY SON'S FIRST INTERVIEW, he didn't think he needed to prepare because he felt that he was a good public speaker. But public speaking, where you mostly memorize, and an interview, where you are expected to answer on the spot, are entirely different. We practiced interviewing a couple of times until he felt comfortable. We also suggested that he ask questions of his interviewer. This went over really well.

—R.K.
PHILADELPHIA, PENNSYLVANIA
1
UNIVERSITY OF PENNSYLVANIA

MAKE SURE YOU VISIT YOUR TOP CHOICES because colleges want to be courted by students. My son was a legacy at his second-choice school. He was overqualified and I was certain he would get in. He applied to nine schools and was accepted at all of them except the legacy school. When I called the school to inquire, they said they rejected him because he never made an official visit. Because he didn't schedule an interview, they just thought that he wasn't that interested.

—ANONYMOUS
NEW YORK, NEW YORK
2
CORNELL UNIVERSITY; DUKE UNIVERSITY

EARLY DECISION IS WRONG IF ...

- Your child is not fully sure of any one school over another;

- You will need to or want to compare financial aid packages;

- You are hoping your child will be awarded a scholarship at one or several schools;

- You see ED as a way of upping the admission odds in the game of college admission;

- You and your child have not visited the campus, as well as other college campuses for comparison.

MY DAUGHTER WANTS TO GO INTO BROADCAST NEWS, so
she sent a reel of some stories she did while she was in
high school. If your child's major is going to be something
related to television, production, or visual arts, then I
would definitely look into this option.

> —ANONYMOUS
> NEW YORK, NEW YORK
> 2
> BOSTON UNIVERSITY; GEORGETOWN UNIVERSITY

• • • • • • • •

*I was told, "If you smell turkey, you're too
late." Get your applications in by November
1. It really will help the family have a nice
Thanksgiving if the pressure is off.*

> —KATHY THOMAS
> DALLAS, TEXAS
> 1
> TEXAS CHRISTIAN UNIVERSITY

• • • • • • • •

THE COLLEGE PROCESS MUST BE OWNED by the student.
The parent has an executive or administrative role and
the college counselor is really a support person.

> —SHARON
> PHILADELPHIA, PENNSYLVANIA
> 2
> WESLEYAN UNIVERSITY; WASHINGTON & LEE UNIVERSITY

I GAVE MY SON SOME GOOD HARD PUSHES during the college application process. Once my son realized he wanted to go to school in Pennsylvania, I pushed him to do all the applications for schools there that met his criteria. We could have peace of mind with the mere $30 that it cost to submit.

—ROBIN MALKI
WEST ORANGE, NEW JERSEY
1
BLOOMSBURG UNIVERSITY

* * * * * * * *

MY HUSBAND AND I WATCHED the deadlines and made sure they were met, but other than that, our kids completed their applications on their own. They're going to have to do their own work once they're at school, and the application process is a good time to start learning how to handle that kind of responsibility.

—JENNIFER
CINCINNATI, OHIO
1
MIAMI UNIVERSITY OF OHIO

* * * * * * * *

MY DAUGHTER HAD A REALLY GOOD academic record and her SAT scores were also good. But we didn't know if that was enough. We really tried to focus on making her essays stand out as she completed each application. So far, it's worked! She's been accepted to five colleges and they are all top universities.

—T.W.
LITHONIA, GEORGIA
1
UNDECIDED

SUPPLEMENTARY MATERIAL

Don't be lured into one of the biggest psychological traps in the college application form—supplementary material. This fairly standard invitation to submit extra work implies that there's more that can be done to influence the individual admissions decision. It may subtly pressure your child to come up with creative things to send that are not appropriate. A student may not feel he has done all he can without sending "something."

Convince your child (and yourself) that simply crossing the t's and dotting the i's on the application is all that is required; it is really true. A good applicant is admitted based on the regular criteria. Your child gets full credit for all the activities listed on the application—admissions officers know how to interpret them by the time commitment and length of commitment—and frankly, if your child is committed to an activity, his degree of talent (even if zero) doesn't matter.

If, in spite of this assurance, your child feels he must submit supplementary material, make sure it isn't covered in the following list:

- Doodled drawings, if art is a hobby
- Full scientific papers. Give the summary elsewhere in the application.
- CD's of music, unless your child is truly a prodigy
- Anything edible
- Anything requiring assembly or explanation

MY SON WAS JUST ABOUT TO HIT the 'send' button to turn in his applications and I asked him if I could look them over. I found two typos on the application that I was able to correct. The counselors are focused on the essays and sometimes forget to look over the actual applications. You hire them to be a *second* set of eyes; you have to be the first.

—D.G.
SANTA MONICA, CALIFORNIA
🎓 2
🏛 DREXEL UNIVERSITY; UNIVERSITY OF PENNSYLVANIA

• • • • • • • •

THERE'S SO MUCH PAPERWORK INVOLVED; if you don't keep it organized you'll just go nuts. We kept a box filled with files labeled for each school we applied to, and every piece of correspondence we got from those schools went immediately in that box. That way, if I wanted to know the status of something or the date it arrived, the official hard copies were right there in one place.

—REBECCA TOMAN
CANFIELD, OHIO
🎓 2
🏛 UNIVERSITY OF CINCINNATI; XAVIER UNIVERSITY

• • • • • • • •

MY DAUGHTER GROUPED HER ACTIVITIES by interest instead of listing them chronologically. It looked more serious that way.

—GRETA TAYLOR
BROOKLYN, NEW YORK
🎓 2
🏛 GOUCHER COLLEGE; BARD COLLEGE

> *It's like being a manager. Think of your child as the executive and yourself as the administrative assistant.*
>
> —C.T.
> SANTA MONICA, CALIFORNIA
> 🏛 SIMMONS COLLEGE; CORNELL UNIVERSITY

I LITERALLY INTERVIEWED MY SON and then we sat down together and wrote the résumé. I didn't just say he played soccer for four years. We wrote about the teamwork and expounded on what he learned from the experience. We determined his best assets and listed those attributes at the top of the résumé. We did it as if for a job interview.

—KATHY THOMAS
DALLAS, TEXAS
☗ 1
TEXAS CHRISTIAN UNIVERSITY

. . . .

MY SON WAS ADOPTED FROM BRAZIL and our family still maintains ties to Brazil. I'm the director of a nonprofit in Rio and my son's done many fundraisers throughout the years. This past summer he went to volunteer at the orphanage in Rio. He wanted to volunteer, of course, so it was just a perk that it looked good on the college application. We highlighted this in his application.

—ROBIN MALKI
WEST ORANGE, NEW JERSEY
☗ 1
BLOOMSBURG UNIVERSITY

. . . .

MY HUSBAND SET UP a project-management Web site for the applications. We'd all log on and complete our assigned tasks.

—N.
NEW YORK, NEW YORK
☗ 1
CARLETON COLLEGE

YOU KNOW THE WHOLE THING is out of hand when applying for college has taken up your child's life and he drops things that were important to him before the process began. If he wants to quit teams he loved being on; if he isn't seeing his friends; if the family stops doing usual things, like eating meals together or going to religious services, then it's too much.

—TERESA OEFINGER
PETALUMA, CALIFORNIA
♉ 1
UNIVERSITY OF CALIFORNIA, DAVIS

. . . .

I HAD TO BE THE HEAVY AND FORCE my son to fill out the applications. He wanted to go to college, but in senior year there was always something more fun for him to do. It is very hard to pin them down. I had to kick one of his friends out the door on a Sunday afternoon to make him sit down at the computer and fill out the forms.

—KATHY THOMAS
DALLAS, TEXAS
♉ 1
TEXAS CHRISTIAN UNIVERSITY

Overboard! Knowing How Far Is Too Far

How much are you going to assist your child with his application? How much leeway are you going to give him to accomplish all the tasks? And what if your child is not the most motivated in the world—can you stand by and just watch? Is there a clear boundary line between what you can and what you must not do for your child?

There really are some concrete rules for appropriate parental behavior when it comes to filling out the applications, crafting the essays, and communicating with the schools. Admissions officers have heard from guidance counselors and have read in too many Internet blogs that parents are taking increased—and inappropriate—roles in their children's applications. And you know an issue has gone too far if it garners media attention and comes with its own special term, like "helicopter parent." Colleges have begun to help educate parents about their real role in the application process; it's something they never imagined needing to do.

Many parents may think there's nothing wrong, and certainly nothing dangerous, in "helping." You are the parent; you're about to pay a fortune for this education; you know your child and, usually, what is best for him. The slippery slope occurs when a child fails to take responsibility for himself and comes to a point when an application is no longer his own. Admissions offices can smell these applications a mile away, and it truly endangers your child's chance of admission. After all, would you hire someone in your office if you knew he had not written his own resume and cover letter?

So, here is a hard and fast rule for you. If you break it, you are going too far, doing something wrong, and and/or hurting your child. Getting caught doing any of these things can easily sideline your child's application: if you ever find yourself signing your child's name, writing in his voice, speaking in his stead, contacting every alumnus you can find, or contacting the admissions office on a regular basis, you've gone overboard.

MY HUSBAND AND I were on a college tour with our daughter: right up in front, first in the group to raise our hands and ask questions, so close to the tour guide that when she stopped we almost bumped into her. Our daughter gradually sank back into the group until she had completely distanced herself from us and was at the very end. We realized then that we were way too into it and that we needed to back off.

—TERESA OEFINGER
PETALUMA, CALIFORNIA
1
UNIVERSITY OF CALIFORNIA, DAVIS

• • • • • • • • •

PARENTS GO OVERBOARD when they keep mentioning the same thing over and over so that it becomes more of a task rather than something that a student looks for as the nicest time in their life. You don't want to irritate your child by telling them what they should do and what they shouldn't do. A picture should be painted about what college really means—that it will be the best time of their lives and an unbelievably incredible experience to look forward to.

—R.F.
LITHONIA, GEORGIA
3
DUKE UNIVERSITY; UNIVERSITY OF MIAMI(2)

SOME PARENTS ACTUALLY WRITE ESSAYS, send e-mails to schools in the name of the student, fill out applications, and push schools. Parents who have neither the time nor the interest hire consultants to craft their child's accomplishments so they will be presented in a more interesting light. I believe that supporting my children has been an ongoing process since they were born. The most influence I had on my son and daughter was brainstorming possible essay topics. Also, I helped with proofreading.

—SHARON
PHILADELPHIA, PENNSYLVANIA
2
WESLEYAN UNIVERSITY; WASHINGTON & LEE UNIVERSITY

. . . .

MY DAUGHTER WAS ON A TRIP to Hawaii and I was given strict orders not to open anything that came in the mail. You know if it's a thick envelope they got in and if it's a thin envelope you just don't know. So I was holding things up to the light, and trying to figure out whether or not the thick envelopes were acceptance letters or rejection letters. If it was a window envelope I would pull the window up to see if I could get a glimpse of a word that would indicate whether or not she got in. Some of the acceptances come online; I knew her passwords, but I knew I couldn't check.

—ANONYMOUS
LOS ANGELES, CALIFORNIA
1
UNIVERSITY OF WASHINGTON

I realized I went a bit overboard when I called up the college and the receptionist said, "Hi Gloria, what can I do for you today?"

—G.V.
HOUSTON, TEXAS
UNIVERSITY OF TEXAS, AUSTIN; UNIVERSITY OF MICHIGAN

TO GET THE JOB DONE

M ost people thought I went way over the top when it came to the application process, but I thought everything I did was necessary. I spent a full day looking at all of the essay questions and thought about all of the different possible topics. I told my daughter, "This essay is similar to this." I made this huge chart and said, "For example, this one for Stanford can be used for this one at Cornell." I also made a chart for deadlines. I organized the teacher and counselor recommendations by making packets to send to each teacher and stamped postcards that the colleges could send back to me. I had a whole file box that I kept organized; each college had its own folder with correspondence. I would remind my daughter to e-mail coaches back. I set up interviews for my daughter. I opened the mail and put stuff on the calendar. I used to even e-mail stuff under her name; with her permission, I would write some people back as my daughter and say, "OK, we'll meet you on such and such a date." The only thing she really had to do on her own was write her essays.

—C.T.
SANTA MONICA, CALIFORNIA
♟ 2
🏛 SIMMONS COLLEGE; CORNELL UNIVERSITY

THE DEFINITION OF OVERBOARD

Overboard is screaming, threatening, warning, "You'll put me in my grave!" Anything short of that is not overboard, especially as the application deadline nears and the student (as my son did) "ruminates"—which I defined as *sitting in his room!* In general, if nagging and stalking occurs triweekly or less, that is not overboard. I did not fill out my kids' applications nor did I write their essays for them (but I wanted to). My job was overseer and worrier. I worried for them so they would not have to. I also drew a line on the map to indicate what states they were allowed to reside in. I gave them "tips" about the religious makeup of certain areas, the distance from home, and the schools that, to me, were "prestigious" and/or acceptable.

—MIRIAM SILVERMAN
ELKINS PARK, PENNSYLVANIA
🎓 2
🏛 SYRACUSE UNIVERSITY; UNIVERSITY OF MARYLAND

MY SON WANTED TO HANDLE the entire application process on his own and I knew he was completely capable, but my own fears and insecurities got the best of me. He didn't want to talk about anything or show me any of his essays and completed applications. So to satisfy my curiosity, I went through his things when he was out of town for a weekend. My son actually anticipated this and totally set me up. He left an essay on top of his pile that was titled, "My Mother Is Crazy." It wasn't what he turned in with his applications but he clearly communicated to me how disturbed he was by his overbearing mother.

—J.M.
RENO, NEVADA
🎓 1
🏛 UNIVERSITY OF PENNSYLVANIA

• • • • • • • •

A WOMAN WHO WOULD BE a determining factor in my daughter's university admission lived a block away from us. When I found out, I began to walk my dogs by her house a few times a day. After a few weeks, I finally saw her and struck up a conversation. I told her that my daughter was going to apply to college that year; the look on her face was one of disgust. She realized that my only interest in her was for what she could do for my daughter. I was so embarrassed and mad at myself for being such a fool.

—MELISSA
LOS ANGELES, CALIFORNIA
🎓 1
🏛 UNIVERSITY OF CALIFORNIA, SAN DIEGO

> *I wouldn't ask the admissions officer out for a beer. Asking for an update near or just after a key date seems to be OK, though.*
>
> —ANDY
> HIGHLANDS RANCH,
> COLORADO
> 🏛 UNDECIDED

YOU ARE NOT THE APPLICANT

Without a doubt, applying to college is a family event. It takes a family's commitment to hard work and studying; chauffeuring to and support at activities; school visits and tours; application work; and of course, a financial investment.

Yes, you are footing the bill, and yes, this is your emotional investment, too, but if you're researching colleges for him, writing to admissions officers because he is "too busy" or calling offices asking about "*our* application" you are making a mistake. This behavior will hobble your child's ability to think for himself, advocate for himself, and know how to take care of himself. You do not want a dependent child; of course you want him to grow and mature, so let him take responsibility for himself. Admissions officers want to hear from the applicants, not the parents. Of course, if you yourself have questions, it is appropriate to ask them; but if you are doing something in your child's stead, you've gone overboard. Avoid behavior that will lead to an unhealthy dependency on you later on and prevent your child from maximizing his college years in the very near future.

AO'S ARE PROS

Admissions officers are your peers (unless they are brand-new, 21-year-old college graduates) and it is easy to feel that you are on the same page with them. It can lead you to think that if you can get to know them, you might influence your child's admission decision. In theory, this could work, but it always backfires.

When talking to parents, admissions officers throw up a subtle, internal defensive shield: they will speak with you adult-to-adult, but this is still a political process.

Bringing gifts is a bad idea. Gifts are appropriate, if ever, only after your child has been admitted and has had a great deal of correspondence with the admissions officer. Gifts are for saying thanks, afterwards.

Inviting admissions officers to dinner is not appropriate when they are traveling in your area. Admissions officers cannot appear to be partial: they cannot spend time with you outside this process in any social way, especially in any way related to money.

After your child is admitted, see how much you are still motivated to be friends with the admissions officer. You will most likely have forgotten about it.

A PARENT LEARNS A LESSON

My daughter wrote a surreal essay to send to her first-choice college. She wanted to be creative, but it came across more like she might be on drugs. Her father and I told her she needed to rework it, but she was quite confident that it showed her uniqueness and sent it off. She wasn't accepted, and I'm pretty sure that the essay was at least part of the reason. Subsequently, she wrote another essay for another college. It was similarly cryptic, and again I told her she needed to rework it. She didn't necessarily agree, but she became unsure of her abilities based on her first experience so she went along with me. I made major changes and found the process thrilling and gratifying as the essay took shape. I tinkered, nipped and tucked over a period of days, and thought "Hey! Maybe I'll get into college one day!" It became a personal challenge. In retrospect, I felt it was cheating, but more than that, I saw that she felt devalued by what I had done. As tempting as it might be to step in, just give your observations, and stick to objective things like spelling and grammar. Beyond that, you're doing more harm than good.

—ANONYMOUS
EASTON, PENNSYLVANIA
🏆 1
🏛 TUFTS UNIVERSITY

Applications Finished! Now for the Wait

The envelopes are mailed, the applications were sent via the Internet. There are no more tests to take, no more essays to write, and no more pressure—what is done is done. The quiet, however, can seem just as horrible as the scramble.

How do you cope with the great unknown? Suddenly, there's time for schoolwork, friends, and activities again. You get your life back, too, but what do you do now to pass the time? Take the opportunity to focus on your family. Without the test-prep classes and essay writing, your child will have more time to spend with you: take advantage of this new, rare moment.

You can also take this time to map out your potential decisions, visit colleges, and prepare for the interviews for which your child may be invited. Keep asking questions of the colleges so that when decision time arrives, your child will be able to make his choice within the month's time frame required. This is especially important if he has applied to a large number of schools with relatively little information about them.

Here's a valuable gift you can give your child: keep the appropriate pressure on him to finish high school strongly. It can be a critical mistake for him to succumb to senioritis. Colleges, especially the most competitive schools, are looking at every grade earned, and a bad semester could jeopardize admission. Help your child finish well and show him how to gracefully power through that last semester. It's hard to keep up the pace to the end, but it's worth it.

I WAS NERVOUS BUT TRIED VERY HARD not to let my daughter know. I communicated with my friends about it instead. There are Web sites that are wonderful for that. I also have an online journal, and would share my insecurities with my virtual friends there. That actually helped me a lot in getting through those weeks. Also, my daughter has had some rejections in her life, and has always been very resilient. That made me know that she would survive whatever the decisions were.

—SUSAN
NEW ENGLAND
🎓 1
🏛 BROWN UNIVERSITY

• • • • • • • •

BY THE TIME MY DAUGHTER was a senior in high school, she had a lot of free time on her hands, so I registered her at a community college to take some first-year English and math classes. The benefits to doing this are many: First, why pay $700 for a class at the university level when you can pay $35 at a community college. Second, your child can get some classes out of the way and maybe make her freshman year a little less stressful. And last, it keeps your kids out of trouble during that lull in their senior year, or it just keeps them from spending too many hours on the computer or in front of the television.

—LAURIE BRESNICK
BEVERLY HILLS, CALIFORNIA
🎓 1
🏛 UNIVERSITY OF ARIZONA

AFTER MY DAUGHTER TURNED in her applications, the waiting was unbearable for her. I think we talked about college at least 10 times a day. When her friends came over after school, it's all she talked about. She signed up to some college forums where other students vented about the waiting process. I don't know if it was a good idea for her to sign up to those forums. Many applicants posted things like, "What do you think my chances are of getting into this college?" Then they would list their scores, while other students would make guesses at their chances. This depressed my daughter immensely. Five postings assured her that she wouldn't get into most of the schools she applied to, and she got into them all.

—MELISSA
LOS ANGELES, CALIFORNIA
1
UNIVERSITY OF CALIFORNIA, SAN DIEGO

Once the college applications were in, we all felt a sense of relief. This experience was exciting. I remember being full of hope and excitement!

—SHARON
PHILADELPHIA, PENNSYLVANIA
WESLEYAN UNIVERSITY, WASHINGTON & LEE UNIVERSITY

• • • • • • • •

MY DAUGHTER COMPLETED A HIGH SCHOOL television project after she submitted her college application. The project was amazing and since she was trying to get into a media program, I thought she should send in the project as a supplement to her application and materials already sent. I didn't know if this was allowed, so we called the schools she applied to, and only one said we could do it. I have no idea if it put her over the edge or anything, but she did get accepted there.

—JANE
SCOTTSDALE, ARIZONA
1
UNIVERSITY OF MIAMI

A PARENT'S OPINION

Early action is the best thing that ever happened to our family. I praise Stanford and Yale for continuing the program and do not agree with Harvard and Princeton for their decision to do away with it. Our son had the kind of application that made him a contender everywhere—not a guaranteed sure thing, but he definitely had a good chance of getting into top schools. When the application season rolled around, considering everything, he applied to Stanford early action. If he had been turned down or deferred, no harm done. He got in and it made his holiday season a wonderful thing. The decision wasn't binding, but now he had time to think about whether or not he should take the rest of the admissions season off. Since he was already guaranteed admission to a school he really wanted to attend, he decided to forgo applying to his safety schools and sent in applications to three top schools on his list that he felt were equal to Stanford. He ended up getting into one, rejected at one and wait-listed at the other. Now he had a choice to go to the East Coast or Stanford; he chose Stanford. But by doing it this way, he avoided a lot of stress that students applying during the regular season had to go through.

—Anonymous
Portland, Oregon
1
Stanford University

MESSAGE: WE LOVE YOU

One of the biggest challenges in the college admissions process today: surviving the decision period with self-esteem intact. The brand-name school has become a symbol not only of a child's success but also of your success as a parent: you raised a "good" kid and you did a "good" job if he was admitted to a top school. This is not the truth, of course, but even if you know better, pressure from your adult peers can color the way you perceive things. But neither you nor your child is a failure in any way if rejected from a favorite school. You will not lose face at the next neighborhood cocktail party.

Don't forget that, hard as it is to feel judged by the schools, your children are also afraid of disappointing you, as well as afraid of facing their peers in school after rejections.

The most important message you can communicate to your child during this time is that you have unconditional love for him: as long as he does his best, you believe he will succeed. Let him know that you support his choices and his judgment. It may sound a bit idealistic, but it truly is the best way to help your child through this potentially ego-crushing process.

WAITING TO GET HER ACCEPTANCE LETTERS was the hardest part for my daughter. She was able to find discussion forums on the Internet to talk to other kids who were applying to the same first-choice school as her. She couldn't do that at home because none of her friends chose the same schools. Going online was great. It gave her a much-needed distraction and also helped calm her nerves knowing that kids across the country were experiencing the same worries and fears.

—JOYCE
SCOTTSDALE, ARIZONA
♛ 1
🏛 UNIVERSITY OF MICHIGAN

• • • • • • • •

DON'T ALLOW YOUR CHILD to let up in senior year, even though your child will want to slack off. My friend's daughter failed a class in her last semester and her application was rescinded from the school she had been accepted at. She'd sent in her deposit and she had already gotten an apartment. But when the grades came out, the school said, "Sorry, you can't go here, and you have to reapply next year."

—SUSAN
LOS ANGELES, CALIFORNIA
♛ 1
🏛 UNIVERSITY OF CALIFORNIA, SANTA BARBARA

When you're waiting to hear back from colleges via e-mail, be sure to check your bulk mail or spam mailbox from time to time. Sometimes the college messages end up in the junk mail file.

—V.A.
AUSTIN, TEXAS
🏛 RICE UNIVERSITY; UNIVERSITY OF TEXAS, AUSTIN

MY DAUGHTER HANDED in her applications early, so we had a really long period of time to wait for decisions. Since you know you aren't going to hear from any schools for a while, you kind of put it out of your mind. But as soon as the first letter comes, you start going crazy. It's very tense. Every time the mailman comes you jump.

—C.T.
SANTA MONICA, CALIFORNIA
🎓 2
🏛 SIMMONS COLLEGE; CORNELL UNIVERSITY

• • • • • • • • •

AFTER MY DAUGHTER AND HER FRIENDS submitted their last applications, they all got together for a bonfire and burned everything related to SAT prep, college brochures, etc. They thought it would be a good way for them to ease their suffering during that long waiting period for acceptance letters.

—KAREN
SCOTTSDALE, ARIZONA
🎓 1
🏛 UNIVERSITY OF ARIZONA

Getting the News: Fat Envelopes, Thin Envelopes

March has finally arrived. Your child is hearing from all the schools to which he has applied. Unlike you, he is not waiting for the postman every day—he is probably logging on to the schools' Web sites and finding out the answer the very second the decisions are posted. But the hefty packages are coming via the mail, too, with all of the official information and forms in paper that were posted online.

Of course, there are the thin envelopes as well: "We are sorry ... the applicant pool was extremely competitive this year ... there is not enough room in the class …" Both you and your child may have to handle deep disappointment and dashed dreams. And, potentially just as challenging, your child may hear the decision that he has been wait-listed, with the message, "Hey, we loved you … now hold on … and on and on and on …"

Depending on how well or how poorly things went, your child might need a lot of support. And you may be about to encounter a big test of your parenting abilities. How do you deal with personal disappointment without saddling your child with the feeling that he has failed you? How do you gracefully handle defeat as well as victory? You are about to show your child how an adult behaves—are you prepared?

One of the best ways to prepare for decision time is to always talk conservatively about the application process. As chances of admission become less and less predictable, avoiding calling any school a shoo-in will help—imagine what happens if your child is rejected from that sure thing. Keep telling yourself and him—and believe it—that this process can be unpredictable. Putting all your hopes and dreams into any one school can be dangerous. Wish for the best, brace for the worst, and you will survive the storm.

MY WIFE BECAME FRIENDS with our postman. At that time Princeton sent its early-decision letters via snail mail, so every day when the mail truck pulled up, she ran outside, hoping our son's acceptance letter from Princeton had arrived. On the day it did finally arrive, our mailman changed his route to stop at our house first; he actually made a special trip so that he could hand-deliver the good news.

—ANONYMOUS
2
PRINCETON UNIVERSITY; UNIVERSITY OF PENNSYLVANIA

• • • • • • • •

IT'S NOT SO MUCH FAT AND THIN envelopes anymore; it's more about waiting on the edge of your seat in front of your computer. My son applied early admission to Rice University and I remember when he received an e-mail from the admissions office letting him know the date he would be able to log on to their Web site with a user name and password to find out if he was accepted. It so happened that the date fell on a Friday. We also knew that the systems do not update until the close of business. So my son sat in front of his computer just waiting for that e-mail to arrive. And when it finally came he ran upstairs to get me and we opened it together. And yes, he got in!

—J.M.
MARIETTA, GEORGIA
1
RICE UNIVERSITY

AFTER RECEIVING TWO FAT ENVELOPES with acceptance letters along with a housing packet, she knew that the thin letter from her first choice was a rejection. She didn't even open it. She just ran into her room and cried. So I opened it, and it was a no. I started to shed a tear, but being a man, I just ripped up the paper and dropped it on the floor and began stomping on the pieces like it was one of the people who'd decided to reject my daughter. Then I threw the debris into the garbage. I never wanted her to see a letter that implied she wasn't good enough.

—KEVIN ITSON
CHICAGO, ILLINOIS
1
UNIVERSITY OF ILLINOIS, URBANA-CHAMPAIGN

• • • • • • • •

When my son was accepted to his first-choice college, we were so excited. We had a big celebration, called everybody in the family, had a nice dinner, and thanked all of his teachers for their support.

—GLYNIS RAMOS-MITCHELL
ATLANTA, GEORGIA
2
MIDDLEBURY COLLEGE; UNIVERSITY OF MASSACHUSETTS, AMHERST

THE BENEFITS OF REJECTION

MOST KIDS THINK IT'S THE END of the world when they don't get accepted to their first-choice school, but it's not. I have twins, a boy and a girl, and they applied to the same schools. My son was accepted to his first choice and my daughter ended up having to attend her third-choice school. She was devastated up until the day she left. She is a junior now, and couldn't be happier.

—ANONYMOUS
NEW YORK, NEW YORK
2
BOSTON UNIVERSITY; GEORGETOWN UNIVERSITY

• • • • • • • •

IF YOU DON'T GET ACCEPTED to a place you really want to go, take a gap year and improve the statistics. My daughter was rejected from all of the schools she applied to. Instead of going to a state school or a community college, we decided that she should take a gap year. We set up a timeline with certain goals that she would hit by the time applications season rolled around again. She got an internship and a research position at a lab. Now she was able to include solid work experience on her applications, and letters from her boss. She ended up getting into MIT, which was her first choice the first year she applied.

—ANONYMOUS
1
MASSACHUSETTS INSTITUTE OF TECHNOLOGY

I WAS PRETTY SKEPTICAL about my son's chances of getting into Brown, but that's my personality. He had the qualifications. But he went to a small private school in Atlanta and a lot of students there wanted to go to Brown; there's a mystique about it. I kept thinking, if they knew my son, he would be the one they'd choose. But they don't know him, so why would he be the one? The day they sent out acceptances by e-mail, we all gathered around the computer and he checked his e-mail and he just screamed. We all jumped up and down and yelled and it was exciting. It was a big relief. I also remember crying. My most vivid memory was getting very sad and realizing that he was really leaving.

—ANONYMOUS
ATLANTA, GEORGIA
1
BROWN UNIVERSITY

Just hug them and tell them how great they are; that's all you can do.

—ANONYMOUS
NEW YORK,
NEW YORK
NEW YORK
UNIVERSITY

• • • • • • • •

BOTH OF MY SONS WERE ACCEPTED to their first-choice schools. When my oldest received his letter, we went out to dinner to celebrate. My youngest actually asked me to have a cigar with him! He never had one before, but had seen his older brother smoke one, so when he got accepted to his first choice he said, "Dad, don't you think I deserve a cigar for this?" I just couldn't say no.

—ANONYMOUS
2
PRINCETON UNIVERSITY; UNIVERSITY OF PENNSYLVANIA

I WAS A POSTAL WORKER STALKER. I thought I was going to have a heart attack every time I saw a white postal truck. Thank God many of the envelopes said, "Congratulations" on the outside. Relief would be an understatement when the acceptances came. I am surprised I am not institutionalized right now. I was filled with panic, fear, and anxiety—and that was on the good days of the process.

—MIRIAM SILVERMAN
ELKINS PARK, PENNSYLVANIA
🎓 2
🏫 SYRACUSE UNIVERSITY; UNIVERSITY OF MARYLAND

. . . .

DON'T GET HOOKED ON ONE SCHOOL as the be-all, end-all. My daughter would have done well at many schools. She wound up pursuing her goal of being a vet. She got into her second-choice school for vet school and it turned out great.

—R.F.
ATLANTA, GEORGIA
🎓 1
🏫 UNIVERSITY OF PENNSYLVANIA

. . . .

BUY THEM THE OFFICIAL SCHOOL T-SHIRT or sweatshirt so they can share their acceptance with all of their friends. My daughter wears hers proudly.

—CHRISTINE SHUPALA
CORPUS CHRISTI, TEXAS

PATIENCE AND PERSISTENCE

MY DAUGHTER APPLIED EARLY DECISION to one school and had no other schools on her list. In fact, she didn't even research any other schools. When she was deferred from her one and only school, she was devastated. Her first reaction was, "I'm just not going to go to college." Her second response was, "I'm going to end up in community college with a minimum-wage job." Three weeks from the day she was deferred, she got a phenomenal offer from another school with this amazing scholarship and an offer to study in England for her first semester. She decided to accept the offer, and while we were at that campus accepting her scholarship, she found out that she got into the school that deferred her. She ended up accepting her first choice. I think the hardest part of a deferral and a rejected application are the feelings they drum up—like being last to be picked for a game, or not being asked to a dance or party. So you have to help them to put those "devastated" feelings aside, and do things that will make them feel successful.

—TERRY
IRVINE, CALIFORNIA
🎓 1
🏛 MOUNT HOLYOKE COLLEGE

FROM THE BEGINNING, OUR DAUGHTER WANTED to go to University of Florida. She did not get in. That was extremely disappointing, for her as well as for us. The parents are part of the process. We drove five hours to appeal the university's decision. People told us, "You're wasting your time." But we went, and we spoke to people at the school admissions office. Our daughter had a meeting with them and still did not get into the school. It was very hard. We gave her a lot of encouragement and support. We also had to tell her that you don't always get what you want in life and you need to learn how to make it work. So she did a year at junior college. After that, she transferred to Boston University. She did well there but she still wanted to go to UF. She applied and got in. She ultimately got what she wanted.

—MARLA
BOCA RATON, FLORIDA
2
UNIVERSITY OF FLORIDA; FLORIDA STATE UNIVERSITY

WHEN MY DAUGHTER COULDN'T DECIDE on the seven colleges she'd been accepted to, I bought car decals from each, put them in a brown paper bag and told her to reach in with her eyes closed and pick one. Whichever one came out was where she was going!

—BELINDA DEYTON
MCDONOUGH, GEORGIA
1
DUKE UNIVERSITY

• • • • • • • •

Don't ever use the phrase, "I am sure you will get in." When my daughter was rejected from her top-choice school, she felt like she'd disappointed me.

—ANONYMOUS
NEW YORK, NEW YORK
2
NEW YORK UNIVERSITY

• • • • • • • •

IT WAS REALLY EASY FOR MY DAUGHTER to make her final decision. Most of the schools she applied to offered her financial aid, but the school she chose offered her full room and board, and tuition.

—JANET
LAS VEGAS, NEVADA
1
UNIVERSITY OF ARIZONA

MY SON WAS REJECTED from every school he applied to. He basically locked himself in his room for 48 hours; when he finally came out we talked about finding some schools with rolling admissions that were easier to get into. We just told him that things like this happen and there will always be rejections in life and you just have to keep moving forward. We also talked about how when you are mid-career, no one asks you what school you went to. This is the first time in their lives they are scrutinized; it's a new experience for them, and while they think their lives are over, we just have to be there and reassure them that life does go on.

—SANDY
BOSTON, MASSACHUSETTS
1
UNIVERSITY OF MICHIGAN

• • • • • • • • •

THE HARDEST THING WAS MAKING a final decision and then waiting for the acceptance letter. My daughters worried whether they made the right choice. Talk about anxiety attacks. We reminded them that nothing is permanent—one can change majors, transfer to another school or even take time off if necessary. This choice is about the child, not the parent.

—ANN HAALAND
HIGHLAND, NEW YORK
2
GETTYSBURG COLLEGE; QUINNIPIAC UNIVERSITY

It's a race against time, other students, and even the students themselves. The pressure is tremendous.

—ANNETTE
GERMANTOWN,
MARYLAND
JAMES
MADISON
UNIVERSITY;
UNIVERSITY OF
MARYLAND,
COLLEGE PARK

LAST YEAR, MY DAUGHTER APPLIED early decision to Columbia. She freaked out on the day decisions were being e-mailed and she couldn't even go to school. She ended up getting deferred and cried that entire night. I tried to reassure her that she would get in somewhere, maybe even Columbia. Then it came time for the regular decisions, and she was wait-listed at several of her choices. But the good news was she got into Cornell! It was a tough road and emotions were high. As parents there is really nothing you can do except be there to listen and keep telling them that there is a school for everyone and at least one will take them.

—ANONYMOUS
NEW YORK, NEW YORK
2
CORNELL UNIVERSITY; DUKE UNIVERSITY

• • • • • • • •

OUR SON HAD TO CHOOSE between UCLA and Claremont McKenna College. He had always been an athlete and wanted to continue playing golf in college. One of the reasons he ended up choosing Claremont was that because it was a smaller school, he was guaranteed a place on the golf team. At UCLA there was no guarantee.

—MARY
TIBURON, CALIFORNIA
2
COLORADO UNIVERSITY, BOULDER;
CLAREMONT MCKENNA COLLEGE

HARVARD—OR A SCARF?

My daughter was working part time, and on that day she was out of work at 3 p.m., and the e-mail notifications were coming in after 5 p.m. She asked if I would pick her up and take her out to do something. She said, "Mom, I want to go get this scarf." I initially told her that I wasn't going to get her a scarf because her birthday was a month away and I would get it for her then. She said, "I want today to be the day I got my scarf, not the day I got rejected from a bunch of schools." How could I say no? So I got her the scarf.

We got home a little before six and she immediately ran to her computer. I wasn't allowed to be anywhere near. Then I heard a screech. It was a sound I never heard from my daughter; a really strange sound. She said, "Mom, you have to read this!" It was an acceptance from Harvard! The funny part is that after she was done I told her to go get her scarf, and I took it back. I said, "Today does not need to be the day you got a scarf; today is the day you got into Harvard. You can get the scarf next month for your birthday."

—L.L.
GLOBAL NOMAD
2
HARVARD UNIVERSITY; BROWN UNIVERSITY

WE REALLY WANTED OUR SON to go to San Luis Obispo and I was 95 percent sure he was going to go there. But he picked University of Arizona instead. The day he told me he was going to Arizona I cried. I couldn't even talk to him and I left the house and went for a run. His decision was difficult for us to accept because we thought his motivation for going there was wrong; but ultimately we had to accept that it was his decision.

—LAURA
ESCONDIDO, CALIFORNIA
1
UNIVERSITY OF ARIZONA

• • • • • • • • •

THE KIDS CHANGE SO MUCH from the time when they have to apply early to the time when they decide where they want to go. There's still so much going on in their lives. Our son had a very good friend at Williams College, a beautiful place. It's 15 minutes from skiing. They had a theater program, and our son had an interest in that. He and two other kids applied early to Williams; all were deferred. But as soon as he found out he was accepted at Brown, he said, "That's where I'm going." In the long run, we were relieved he didn't get in early to Williams. He has said, "I'm so happy at Brown. This is a great place for me."

—ANONYMOUS
BROOKLYN, NEW YORK
1
BROWN UNIVERSITY

WHEN MY DAUGHTER DIDN'T GET into her top choice, I had her make a list of three things that her top school had to offer. Then I had her write down three negatives regarding her top choice. Ultimately, we were able to find another school with all of the positive attributes she was seeking and only one of the negatives.

—ANONYMOUS
CHICAGO, ILLINOIS
🛡 2
BOSTON UNIVERSITY; DUKE UNIVERSITY

• • • • • • • •

WHEN MY SON WAS ACCEPTED to his first-choice school, I cried. He was out of town when the acceptance letter came in, so my husband and I went out to dinner to celebrate for him. When he came back from his trip, we surprised him with a laptop computer.

—L.R.
SCOTTSDALE, ARIZONA
🛡 1
UNIVERSITY OF CALIFORNIA, BERKELEY

• • • • • • • •

YOU REALLY HAVE TO MAKE SURE that they consider alternatives. I asked my daughter questions like, "If New York City was suddenly destroyed by a meteor, what other city could you see yourself living in?" Or, "If you suddenly had developed ear problems, and couldn't fly, what schools in California could you see yourself going to?"

—T.M.
SAN FRANCISCO, CALIFORNIA
🛡 1

AMAZING

My daughter was accepted at 13 of the 14 schools she applied to. She also got into Yale, so in the end it was between Rhodes College and Yale. It was the dream school that everyone wants versus a fine school in Memphis that no one has heard of. One would cost over $100,000 after the aid she received, and the other was free. When she got the money for Rhodes, she decided within 24 hours that she wanted to forgo Yale, but I wouldn't let her make the call. She knew she wanted to go to medical school, so she was worried about accumulating too much debt. I made her wait a week to really think about things. She finally said, "Dad, you keep thinking I'm going to come to you in four years and say that I can't believe I didn't go to Yale, when what I see is ten years from now being stuck with $250,000 worth of debt from medical school and undergraduate school, and then having to choose a job in the money-making sector rather than the public sector or charity work." Right at that moment, I said, "Go make that call," because I knew that Rhodes was where she wanted to be.

—TOM
WACO, TEXAS
1
RHODES COLLEGE

EVEN IF YOU BELIEVE WITHOUT A DOUBT that your child will get into his or her first-choice school, make sure you build up the others, too. My daughter really wanted to get into Stanford, but she didn't. She was really disappointed, partly because I had contributed to making her think that it was more important than it really was. I talked about it all of the time. We gave her the feeling that she would be failing if she didn't get in.

—KAREN BARCHAS
TRUCKEE, CALIFORNIA
🎓 1
🏛 UNIVERSITY OF CALIFORNIA, BERKELEY

· · · · · · · · ·

WHEN IT CAME DOWN to choosing a college, affordability was the most important. I believe all colleges pretty much give the same education; some just made a name for themselves, while others are state schools. It's just what the student puts into it. My daughter received a four-year scholarship to Grand Valley State University. No other school gave her that. Therefore, there was nothing to narrow down. The question was, "When does school start?"

Consider

—MONICA FRAZIER
CHICAGO, ILLINOIS
🎓 1
🏛 GRAND VALLEY STATE UNIVERSITY

Even if they don't get into every school, it doesn't matter. You only need one.

—D.F.
LITHONIA,
GEORGIA
DUKE
UNIVERSITY;
UNIVERSITY OF
MIAMI (2)

MY DAUGHTER'S CHOICE CAME DOWN to two state schools. I thought that would be the easy part, but it was the worst part of all. Her decision came down to one nagging question: "Do I want to go far away, or do I want to stay nearby?" She kept going back and forth. One school was five hours away, while another was one hour away. There were so many reasons to stay: be closer to family and friends; be near the big city; less travel. She also had a thousand reasons to be far away: a new environment; warmer weather; nice road trips; closer to another state. It just went on and on, and I thought I was going to die of repeated question syndrome. One month before school started, my indecisive daughter picked the school that was closer to home. That's the school I thought I wanted too—until she came home every weekend and wanted her clothes washed.

—KEVIN ITSON
CHICAGO, ILLINOIS
1
UNIVERSITY OF ILLINOIS, URBANA-CHAMPAIGN

• • • • • • • • •

I THINK THERE IS A POINT where you just have to let your kids be and make their own decisions. You guide them and give them the information they need to succeed, but ultimately they will do what they want.

—JANET
LAS VEGAS, NEVADA
1
UNIVERSITY OF ARIZONA

My daughter received two acceptances. I considered buying her sweatshirts for the two schools, but the prices were steep. And since we will have a tuition bill coming in a few months, who has the money?

—SUSAN
NEW ENGLAND
🏺 1
🏛 BROWN UNIVERSITY

• • • • • • • • •

MY OLDEST DAUGHTER APPLIED early decision to Brown and was deferred. It's really stressful for them to have to wait after their first deferment or rejection. My younger daughter applied to Cornell early decision, but because of what happened to my first daughter, I had the younger one apply to Pennsylvania State and University of Michigan. Both schools have rolling admissions, I knew she would get into them, so if she didn't get into Cornell she would at least have some positive feedback. Just make sure they apply early, so that they get in early in the season.

—ANONYMOUS
NORTH POTOMAC, MARYLAND
🏺 2
🏛 BRANDEIS UNIVERSITY; CORNELL UNIVERSITY

MAKING THE FINAL DECISION

It always amazes admissions professionals how the decisions about university selection are made. Just as often as students make careful, reasoned, decisions about their matches, they make rather whimsical decisions based on unpredictable events: they visited campus on a rainy day and it colored their view about the school's atmosphere, or perhaps they have a friend of a friend currently studying somewhere who says that a college is "cool."

You've applied many criteria in narrowing down your application choices. Now that you are choosing among admission offers, though, broad categories such as academic level, and possibly size and location, have been decided. This next decision round can become more a matter of gut feeling than logic. Nonetheless, there are some rational tools you can use to evaluate the choices.

ATMOSPHERE: First and foremost, you are seeking to place your child where he will be happy and therefore succeed. Academically, you want to choose the school offering the necessary majors, as well as a range of academic strengths in case, as so often happens, he wants to change his mind. Your child may want a place where he is among the smartest, or a place where he is challenged by his peers and may have to work harder;

achieving academically will be easier in the right class-room. The school should also be a match for your child's personality. For example, if your child likes crowds, don't push the tiny suburban or rural school. Your child needs a core group like himself and the comfort to feel free to express himself.

COST: After weighing the pros and cons of your financial packages, and/or the pros and cons of the state school at the lower cost versus the private school, choose a school which you will be able to afford without making such a sacrifice that it hurts too much and adds too much pressure on both you and your child.

LOGISTICS: Consider what you value as a family in location and communication patterns. How far away is the school? Is it OK to fly between your home and the college? Does your child need to be close to home and want to come home on weekends? What is the comfortable distance you want between yourselves: a car ride, a phone call, or a couple of time zones away? Be clear about this factor—it can color the whole family's experience for four (or more) years.

WHAT DO YOU STAND FOR?

The college admissions process is a wonderful opportunity to model your family's values and behavior. Do you encourage your daughter to lie in her application (for example, create a leadership title in her favorite organization to make herself look better)? Do you act as if it is OK to apply to more than one school on a binding early decision basis? Do you encourage your son to play games of flattery just to collect a trophy admission letter, knowing that he will certainly turn down the offer? Do you send in a deposit at more than one school because you and your child simply cannot decide which school he wants, when you are required to commit to one—and only one—school? Do you back out on a school (to which you have sent an admissions deposit) without warning or explanation in the spring or summer before entry?

By doing any of these things, you are telling your child that he should be self-centered and do anything to get ahead in life; that it is OK to be irresponsible to others; and that it is OK to break rules. Your actions in these moments are very powerful. A good parent puts a lot of responsibility on the child to act responsibly—and that is the best tool you can bestow to prepare and empower him for his college career and beyond.

SPREADSHEETS ARE WONDERFUL TOOLS when it comes to comparing schools, financial awards, tuition/room/board, travel expenses, and pros and cons. The selection process is much easier when you see the information laid out side by side. Our son set up a spreadsheet with all of the schools he had applied to. As applications were sent out and letters of acceptance came in, he made notes of the school, how long it took for a response, the scholarship offers, unusual expenses that are often overlooked (storage, travel, etc.), and notations about the visit. With this process, he trimmed down a list of seven schools one by one until he came to his final decision.

—ANONYMOUS
KENT, WASHINGTON
2
WASHINGTON STATE UNIVERSITY; UNIVERSITY OF WASHINGTON

MY SON WAS RECRUITED by many of the Ivy League schools. He narrowed down his choice based on what he wanted to do when he graduated, which was business. He did his own research to come to a conclusion. I know that all kids are different, but if you have a child like mine who is independent and intelligent, there is no need for much hand-holding. When they go out in the world, they are going to need to rely on themselves, so why not start now?

—ANONYMOUS
LAS VEGAS, NEVADA
1
HARVARD UNIVERSITY

REJECTION CAN HURT EVERYONE

Your child got the thin envelope—rejected from his dream school—and your hopes are also dashed. How will you react? Rejection is similar to a grieving process; there are stages to pass, and your strength and health at the end depends on how you are able to progress through these stages of "mourning."

SADNESS/DISAPPOINTMENT: Your heart sinks, knowing that your child will not be on that dream campus in the fall. Your heart breaks for your child's disappointment.

ANGER: You think, "How could they not have taken my amazing child? What were they thinking?"

LETTING GO: You can finally say, "This was not the place for my child. There are other places where she was admitted, and where she will be happy; I want to help her find her place."

Through the difficult first stages, you are most vulnerable to upsetting your children further by the way you react. Here are a few critical mistakes you can make in handling yourself that can prevent your child from moving forward.

MISTAKE #1: Calling admissions officers and yelling at them in your child's presence. An aggressive, angry conversation will achieve nothing (aside from annoying the admissions officer), and it only models poor sportsmanship. This is neither the first nor the last disappointment you will have in your lives. If your child really needs closure and has to ask why, he can make a calm, rational, investigatory phone call—by himself—to the admissions office.

MISTAKE #2: Encouraging your child to open a new campaign for admission. Sending letters and e-mails, having everyone you know contact every office on campus, and returning to the admissions office to fight in person will only waste your child's time and emotional energy and prevent you from moving on to better choices. Admissions decisions are rarely, if ever, reversed. Focus your energies on real possibilities.

MY FIRST DAUGHTER WAS A STRONG STUDENT and an athlete, and decided to apply early decision to a top college. She was encouraged by the coach, who thought she was a good fit for the school. Despite her excellent credentials, she was deferred. She found out that a C+ in AP Calculus the first quarter of her senior year was the reason. Since she had her heart set on this school, she worked very hard in her Calculus course and pulled up her grade. She then wrote a heartfelt letter to the Dean of Admissions, telling him about her struggle with calculus and how his college was still her first choice. In the end she was admitted to five highly selective colleges, including the school that deferred her. I think the letter she wrote definitely helped.

—LUCY RUMACK
BROOKLYN, NEW YORK
1
SWARTHMORE COLLEGE

• • • • • • • •

Consider

THE MOST DIFFICULT TIME FOR US was between April 1 and May 1 of my daughter's senior year. On April 1, you receive most of your acceptance letters. On May 1, you need to choose the school you want to go to. They don't give you that much time.

—T.S.
LOS ANGELES, CALIFORNIA
1
DUKE UNIVERSITY

WRESTLING WITH MY DAUGHTER for three months about what college she would attend made me want to pull her hair out. She wanted to attend a historically black college in Atlanta, meeting African Americans from all over the country and having the experience of living in another state for four years. But the school cost too much. We would have been struggling during school and after graduation. I refused because I didn't want my daughter in debt after college. She kept arguing and said that it would be a good experience and that she didn't mind paying back loans. But I've been there and done that. It has taken me ten years to pay back student loans, which took a toll on my social life. She finally went to a state school. During the trip to campus she was angry, but after a couple of weeks, she apologized and said she was having the time of her life.

—DEBRA
CHICAGO, ILLINOIS
🗑 1
🏛 SOUTHERN ILLINOIS UNIVERSITY; WESTERN ILLINOIS UNIVERSITY

MORE GOOD NEWS

Ninety percent of all college applicants are accepted to their first- or second-choice school, according to recent surveys.

APPLYING TO SCHOOLS IS COSTLY, not only in the sense of the application fee, but also the time and energy it takes to write essays or answer questions, and the tension that comes with waiting to hear from the schools. We limited our kids to applying to no more than ten colleges. Any more than ten can cause confusion and burnout because there's too much to choose from and so little time. A friend of our son's applied to nearly 50 colleges in a quest for the ever-elusive, full-ride academic scholarship. It never materialized and it made the process all the more stressful for him.

—ANONYMOUS
KENT, WASHINGTON
2
WASHINGTON STATE UNIVERSITY; UNIVERSITY OF WASHINGTON

The Hardest Part: Letting Them Go

Whether this is your only, first, or last child, his departure for college is a difficult transition. Your "kid" is about to be an "adult," and begin his independent life. You will not be disappearing from the picture, but this is the moment when his survival skills—and yours—will be put to the test.

In these days of extensive parental involvement, letting go and allowing your child to rise or fall on his own is extra challenging. Take heart: he wants his independence, but you secretly have more influence upon his choices than he cares to admit. Remember this as you prepare for the inevitable conflicts.

The summer before college is just as scary for your child—he is excited, but also nervous about the unknown. Your calm encouragement will make things easier. Consider ways to arm him with extra love, support, and skills. Take a family vacation; teach him how to do laundry; help him set up a bank account; figure out what he needs for his room.

After you move your child into his dorm, when it comes time to part, just go. A clean break is the best for both of you. All the other parents are just as emotional as you are, but take your cue from them about when to drive away.

As with every other part of this process, you'll have to find your own answer about letting your child know your thoughts—is it helpful or harmful for him to know how much you are missing him?

How can you deal with the empty space in your daily life? Take after your child—meet new people, embark on new activities, and find new ways to enrich your life. You finally have time for yourself: Do you remember how good that feels? And if it still doesn't feel good, don't worry: Christmas vacation is just around the corner.

WHAT REMAINS WITH ME constantly is the day I took her to the airport. I drove, and three of her best friends came with us. I let them say their goodbyes first. The four of them were so choked up and had tears in their eyes, and it just melted my heart. At that moment, seeing the deep and solid connections she had with these girls gave me the strength to let her go. I knew that she would find new friends at school that would be able to give her the emotional support she needed in tough times. I knew if she could build friendships like the ones she did in high school that she would not be alone.

—TRACY
CHICAGO, ILLINOIS
1
WASHINGTON UNIVERSITY

• • • • • • • •

BEFORE YOU LEAVE THEM THAT FIRST TIME, define your expectations of how often you're going to communicate and the medium of communication you'll use while they're at school. Even though you're dying to hear about how everything's going, you just can't call them as much as you'd like. We decided to e-mail during the week, and if we wanted to talk on the phone we could do that on weekends. For us, e-mails have worked really well. They let me know enough about what's going on so I'm not dying to call every day.

—DONNA
CINCINNATI, OHIO
2
MIAMI UNIVERSITY

I was crying about my son's departure for college a year before he left.

—ANONYMOUS
ATLANTA,
GEORGIA
BROWN
UNIVERSITY

A FUN GAME MAKES A GREAT parting gift for a freshman going off to school. We gave our daughter a game called Catch Phrase, where players sit in a circle and try to guess different phrases based on others' clues. She asked people to play and it was an immediate, easy, fun way to meet the people around her. They played it for the first week or so. What a great icebreaker!

—LESLIE KUHLMAN
CINCINNATI, OHIO
🚩 1
FRANCISCAN UNIVERSITY OF STEUBENVILLE

• • • • • • • • •

AFTER A ROUGH SUMMER of arguing with my son about curfews, chores, and friends, I was almost relieved to imagine him going thousands of miles away to college in mid-August. But, the day after he left, I went into an unexpected period of mourning; it was two weeks before I could bear to enter his room. When I finally opened his door, the sight jerked me back into reality: The room was a complete pigsty, after he'd sworn he left it clean! Candy wrappers, bottle caps, clothes—even a girl's camisole (!)—were strewn all over the floor. I went straight from grief to anger. Sobbing, picking up dirty socks and wadded-up papers, I worked through my full range of emotions while straightening up that room.

—N.L.
ST. LOUIS, MISSOURI
🚩 2
TRUMAN STATE UNIVERSITY; CALIFORNIA STATE UNIVERSITY, MONTEREY BAY

ALONE AT LAST!

Some couples are shocked to find out that, having put all of their energy into their children and their activities, there is no relationship left with their spouse. When my youngest daughter was a high school senior, I spent that year preparing myself for empty nesting. I renewed my dedication to having a quality relationship with my husband, worked on making sure we had shared interests after she was gone and things to talk about at the dinner table besides her activities. All went as planned; our daughter left for college and things were looking positive. Then our older daughter called to say she would be coming home to live with us for a year so she could save for a house. A month later, she moved in, along with more furniture, clothing, and random belongings. A year later, she moved out, only to be replaced by her oldest sister who needed to move in with her two young children to save money. They have all since moved out: we love them all, wish them well, and hope they all are doing well, someplace else.

—ANNETTE
GERMANTOWN, MARYLAND
👤 2
🏛 JAMES MADISON UNIVERSITY;
UNIVERSITY OF MARYLAND, COLLEGE PARK

THE DROP-OFF SCENE MADE ME LAUGH: all the parents with the Bed, Bath and Beyond bags, bumping into each other. And while the parents are doing all the work carrying stuff in, the child yawns and holds the door for them.

—MARLA
BOCA RATON, FLORIDA
👜 2
🏛 UNIVERSITY OF FLORIDA; FLORIDA STATE UNIVERSITY

• • • • • • • •

Even though it's hard, the separation is good for them; it's part of their growing up, and the separation for you is part of your growing up.

—ANONYMOUS
BEVERLY HILLS, CALIFORNIA
👜 1
🏛 NORTHEASTERN UNIVERSITY

• • • • • • • •

HAVING MY SISTER IN BOULDER was a definite plus when our daughter went there. My sister was there to help my daughter move, and I felt much better knowing someone was there just in case something happened.

—MARY
TIBURON, CALIFORNIA
👜 2
🏛 COLORADO UNIVERSITY AT BOULDER;
CLAREMONT MCKENNA COLLEGE

ONCE THEY'RE AT SCHOOL, it's really hard, but let them initiate all communication, or at least as much as possible. And your kids are more open to communicating with you when they have an opening in their schedule or when they have a need. Having Mom or Dad call every morning is definitely not the best way to keep the lines of communication open.

—V.A.
AUSTIN, TEXAS
2
RICE UNIVERSITY; UNIVERSITY OF TEXAS, AUSTIN

• • • • • • • •

BOTH GIRLS HANDLED their goodbyes differently. Our eldest was surly and rude. She was impatient and demanding and then abruptly "set us free" by telling us we could leave. I was very angry but had to contain my reaction in front of her. I knew she was nervous and she did not want to appear so. And it was important to us to let her do this her way. My husband and I got in the car and I vented at him for the next four hours. Things did get better from there. Our younger daughter's experience was smoother. Perhaps it had to do with her personality or knowing that her sister loved college and she would, too. And as parents, we were three years older. Experience makes it easier.

—ANN HAALAND
HIGHLAND, NEW YORK
2
GETTYSBURG COLLEGE; QUINNIPIAC UNIVERSITY

WHAT YOUR BABY NEEDS

OTHER THAN A LAPTOP and a little bit of clothing, my son didn't really need anything.

> —C.G.
> COOPER CITY, FLORIDA
> 🎓 3
> 🏫 DUKE UNIVERSITY

• • • • • • • •

I RECOMMEND THOSE BED RISERS; they raise the bed about six inches. The storage space under the bed is something to be taken advantage of.

> —ANONYMOUS
> BROOKLYN, NEW YORK
> 🎓 1
> 🏫 BROWN UNIVERSITY

• • • • • • • •

OUR SCHOOL SENT OUT A LIST OF THINGS TO PACK, but I added a couple of items that my son uses all the time. Duct tape is the most important item. There is an all-in-one tool by Leatherman that solves various issues. And another item a lot of schools are requiring now is an allocator, which is a device that automatically switches off your appliances while you are using one so you don't drain your college's electrical system.

> —ANONYMOUS
> RICHMOND, VIRGINIA
> 🎓 1
> 🏫 UNIVERSITY OF VIRGINIA

BEFORE MY SON WENT AWAY I was preoccupied with giving him all sorts of motherly advice that he did not think was necessary. I went over how to do laundry, and what not to put in with the whites. I made him a kit of over-the-counter medicine, I gave him a long list of phone numbers of people he could call if he couldn't find us. Even though he was resistant to it all at first, as time went on he started to realize how all of those tips were coming in handy.

—C.K.
LARKSPUR, CALIFORNIA
1
WHITMAN COLLEGE

• • • • • • • • •

WHEN THEY LEAVE FOR SCHOOL, be sure they pack something—anything—that makes them feel at home. In my family we all sew and quilt, so each kid got a homemade quilt to take to school. It helped them feel comfortable when they got there, and the process of making it helped me prepare for the whole letting-go part.

—REBECCA TOMAN
CANFIELD, OHIO
2
UNIVERSITY OF CINCINNATI; XAVIER UNIVERSITY

WE'D PLANNED TO GO TO HAWAII all my daughter's life, but it was one of those things that finances always deterred us from doing. So right before she left for college we went to Hawaii, got a condo, and hung out for two weeks. And for Christmas I gave her a photo album from our trip. I'm so glad we have that.

—ANONYMOUS
LOS ANGELES, CALIFORNIA
1
UNIVERSITY OF CALIFORNIA, SANTA BARBARA

* * * * * * * * *

AS MY DAUGHTER PREPARED to leave for college, many of my friends asked me how I felt about it. They said things like, "Aren't you sad?" and "I'll bet you'll cry like a baby when she's gone." But that was not at all how I felt. It almost made me feel like a cold-hearted mother for not feeling sorrow. I thought that maybe later it would hit me and I would suddenly break down in tears. So far that hasn't happened. To me it feels very right and natural that at 18 she's out of the house, experiencing life in a new way. There is no sadness in having her away from home, just joy in her accomplishments. I am truly happy that she is moving on in her life and I enjoy the new relationship we share. She has become very good company, and I look forward to her visits.

—ANONYMOUS
EASTON, PENNSYLVANIA
1
TUFTS UNIVERSITY

I loved getting her moved in to her dorm. I cried when I got on the plane, and prayed for her safety as a young woman away from home.

—R.F.
ATLANTA,
GEORGIA
UNIVERSITY
OF PENNSYLVANIA

I DON'T LIKE THAT MY DAUGHTERS are away. I don't like them not being at home, but it's part of life. The hardest thing was saying goodbye to the first one, even though she moved only 20 miles away. When she left, I knew that was the end of it and that we would never all be living together again. Now it is just something to get used to.

—ANTHONY ROMANO
SAN DIEGO, CALIFORNIA
♛ 2
🏛 UNIVERSITY OF CALIFORNIA, SAN DIEGO;
CLAREMONT MCKENNA COLLEGE

• • • • • • • •

DRIVING TO COLLEGE WITH MY DAUGHTER in the backseat, I realized she was a grown woman now, 18 years old and a freshman in college. She did something I never did: she was going to college to fulfill her dreams. I was proud of her, yet she was still my little girl. Those six hours of driving went so fast. All I could remember was getting in the car, and the next minute all her things are jammed in her tiny room. I hugged her and said goodbye. I got back in the van with my husband and she was not there. I smelled the scent of her perfume, and I felt her spirit, but she was gone. I sobbed all the way home. Her dad, who I know was hurting too, remained silent and held my hand. When I got home, I took the one pillow that she left behind, and slept with it in my room for about a month.

—AUDREY DAVIS
CHICAGO, ILLINOIS
♛ 2
🏛 SOUTHERN ILLINOIS UNIVERSITY; ROBERT MORRIS COLLEGE

IT TAKES A VILLAGE

When my son was preparing for college, he said, "Mom, I don't even know how to cook." So a bunch of moms from a group of 14 friends organized a day where all the parents could impart their final words of wisdom.

We came up with a list of all the things the kids need to know before they go away to college. Four of us volunteered our homes. At my house we learned how to clean a toilet—I mean, when else are you going to teach your kid how to clean a toilet? We taught them how to sew a button, how to iron a shirt, how to change a tire, and how to check the fluid in the car. They also learned the essential skill of how to do laundry. A doctor taught them basic first aid.

They learned basic cooking and had to make a salad and cookies. But before they made their salad and cookies someone met them at the grocery store, where they learned how to choose produce and to shop for the ingredients for the meal they were going to prepare. At the end of the day, all of the boys brought their salads and cookies back to our house where my husband taught them how to grill. All the parents came over and we had a potluck that night.

—LAURA
ESCONDIDO, CALIFORNIA
1
UNIVERSITY OF ARIZONA

WE HAVE SIX KIDS and when my son left, the whole dynamic of the family changed. I was devastated. It was the first time I bolted the door before I went to bed, and that wigged me out completely. I used to leave it open because he often came home late. My husband and I drove out with him and moved him in and said goodbye to him outside the dorm. I said, "You've been given this special opportunity that with our financial circumstances we never envisioned you having, so make the most of it." After that I cried.

—BERURAH RUNYON
DERBY, KANSAS
1
DUKE UNIVERSITY

• • • • • • • •

Don't plan on too many warm and fuzzy moments after graduation. I think they go into "I have to separate" mode, and by August you will happily help them pack.

—KATHLEEN RIDER
HYDE PARK, NEW YORK
4
STATE UNIVERSITY OF NEW YORK (2);
FORDHAM UNIVERSITY; QUINNIPIAC UNIVERSITY

MY SON WENT AWAY FOR SIX WEEKS at a time during his last two summers before college, so I thought I would be prepared to say goodbye. I wasn't at all. I'm a single mom and I now live alone. I feel like I have to get a life now. I spend some time on the Web chatting with other parents around the country who are going through the same thing. I also talk to my son once a week and send him care packages. For example, every year since my son was eight, we went to the big Macintosh exhibit in San Francisco; it was the one day a year I allowed him to ditch school. This year he couldn't go, so I went and sent him all the little gadgets I got at the show. On Halloween, which is our favorite holiday, I sent him a big package of candy and decorations for his dorm room. Life goes on, though, and you adjust.

—JILLIAN
OAKLAND, CALIFORNIA
1
CALIFORNIA INSTITUTE OF TECHNOLOGY

It made us proud to see how well we were able to raise him to be independent.

—URSULA ARMSTRONG
MARKESAN, WISCONSIN
STEVENS POINT UNIVERSITY

· · · · · · · · ·

WHEN WE HELPED OUR FIRST CHILD pick out things to bring to college, we started out trying to find things that she wouldn't call us to send. We ended up going way overboard. We packed so much food that by the time she graduated, she still had nonperishable items that we bought that day.

—D.F.
LITHONIA, GEORGIA
3
DUKE UNIVERSITY; UNIVERSITY OF MIAMI (2)

I SEND MY SON CARE PACKAGES every couple of months. He sends me a list of things he needs and I shop and send them to him. Some of the things I've sent are laundry detergent, an iron, batteries, his favorite candy, and a cell phone charger. I know that he is completely capable of getting these items himself, but it's fun for me to do it for him.

—L.R.
SCOTTSDALE, ARIZONA
🎓 1
🏛 UNIVERSITY OF CALIFORNIA, BERKELEY

• • • • • • • • •

I FLEW WITH MY SON TO COLLEGE to help him move in. I was supposed to be there for three days, but ended up staying for two weeks. The move from high school to college is so significant; it just rips your heart out. In retrospect, I should have left when I was supposed to because instead of parting from my son with a hug, a kiss and a few tears, I ended up annoying him and walked away with my tail between my legs. I just couldn't leave him because I knew that I would miss him so much. After the first week, he started making friends with some of the other kids in his dorm and didn't have much time for me. It really hurt, but for some reason I just couldn't pull it together. For other parents who are planning on dropping their kids off, stick to your plans, and let your kids be; they will love you so much more for that.

—J.M.
RENO, NEVADA
🎓 1
🏛 UNIVERSITY OF PENNSYLVANIA

MY YOUNGEST CHILD WAS GETTING COLD FEET by the time school came. When your child's heart isn't totally into it and looking forward to it, that makes it really hard. He's at school now and he calls me all the time. He's a talker and we have lots and lots of phone conversations. I'm not sure though if this helps or hurts in the long run. My son thinks it's helpful to have me to talk to, so for now, I'm not going to deny that to him.

—ANONYMOUS
HICKORY, NORTH CAROLINA
🎓 3
🏫 ELON UNIVERSITY; VIRGINIA INTERMONT COLLEGE; WAKE FOREST UNIVERSITY

• • • • • • • •

MY DAUGHTER BECAME A COMPLETE PAIN in the butt the last two months before she left and we were actually relieved to get rid of her. She was very hyper; she had an attitude. She was really getting stressed and wound up over things that we felt she could have approached with a more relaxed attitude. Now that she's gone though, I miss her. And after going through this process of applying to schools, I realized how much help was not available, so now I spend time helping other kids who are going through what my kids went through. At my son's high school, the word on the street is, don't see the counselor; see me.

—STEPHEN
VANCOUVER, WASHINGTON
🎓 2
🏫 FURMAN UNIVERSITY; OREGON STATE UNIVERSITY

DOCTOR'S PRESCRIPTION

One of the more touching moments with my son was when I took him for his college physical. We went to the pediatrician who had cared for him since he was a baby. Because the doctor no longer sees them after they turn 18, it was my son's last visit. I asked him if he had any parting advice. He was so kind and articulate, having just passed through this phase with his own children. He advised my son to learn to use his time well and not to procrastinate, telling him that he would have much more free time and no one to keep him to a schedule. And he said, "Let your mom do all those little things she needs to do this summer, helping you get ready. It's just her way of letting you go." Then he turned to me and I can't remember exactly what he said (I was pretty choked up by this time), but essentially he said to give my son the space he needed and to not overmanage the process. It was so nice.

—CATHERINE BROWN
UTICA, NEW YORK
1
RENSSELAER POLYTECHNIC INSTITUTE

WHEN YOUR KIDS LEAVE HOME, turn it into something positive and reconnect with your spouse. The first week we were alone, my husband and I met at the grocery store to go shopping. It was so much fun: For the first time in 18 or so years, we were able to buy whatever we wanted without having to consider two additional stomachs. And we walked out of the grocery store with one bag instead of twelve. That night we tried some new recipes, all with foods my daughters wouldn't think of eating, and drank some wine. There were no phones ringing, no one asking to get up from the dinner table, just peace. Take the time to rediscover your relationship. If you make it about new discoveries rather than what you are missing and what you've lost, then it can be amazing.

—L.L.
GLOBAL NOMAD
2
HARVARD UNIVERSITY; BROWN UNIVERSITY

* * * * * * * * *

IT'S DEFINITELY AN ADJUSTMENT, but this is how it should be. It's really healthy. We want them to be functioning and independent members of society. It's time for them to go out and test themselves to see if they can keep it all together; they have to be responsible for their own nutrition, clothing and friendships. This is the time when they become who they really are, how can that be sad?

—J.M.
ARLINGTON, VIRGINIA
2
LEHIGH UNIVERSITY; ELON UNIVERSITY

MY WIFE WAS THRILLED when my son decided to stay on the West Coast. He's just a long car ride away now, and my wife was content knowing that she could show up on campus every once in a while for a visit. Despite the fact that we could just hop in our car any time, his departure came as a shock. He is our only child, so to go from having a three-person family, with a big focus on the prospects of the child, to an empty nest with much less involvement, is pretty serious.

—ANONYMOUS
PORTLAND, OREGON
🎓 1
🏫 STANFORD UNIVERSITY

* * * * * * * *

We told him, "Look, we don't want a phone call from the police, the emergency room, or the academic dean. Those are the three phone calls we don't want. Anything else is probably OK."

—C.G.
COOPER CITY, FLORIDA
🎓 3
🏫 DUKE UNIVERSITY

THE EMOTIONAL SKILLS TOOLBOX

Colleges will provide resources and lists to assist you in purchasing everything from bedding to meal plans, but there are arguably more important things you can do to prepare your child; you can give him a set of emotional skills. Skills for thriving in a new and challenging environment are the most valuable gifts you can give, not only for his college years, but for his future.

Help your child:

- Call to check in and call when lonely, but learn to make decisions on his own;
- Learn to wake up without assistance;
- Learn to take responsibility for strong or weak academic work;
- Prepare to meet new people. He will be exposed to things both fabulous and distasteful; how will he handle both?
- Jump into campus activities. It will enrich his experience, and students always regret not doing enough during the four years.
- Learn how to ask for help—from professors, TAs, and RAs—and know how to find and use campus resources such as offices of Student Life, Religious Life, and Medical Services (including psychological care).

YOU HAVE TO FIND SOME WAY to accept that they might end up at a school over 3,000 miles away. We live in San Francisco and my daughter is leaning toward going to school in New York or Boston. I know I'm not going to see her every night at the dinner table, I know that there's a chance she might meet a boyfriend out there and not come home for the holidays, but I know we will stay close because our family is strong.

> —T.M.
> SAN FRANCISCO, CALIFORNIA
> 🎓 1
> 🏛 UNDECIDED

• • • • • • • •

WE HAD PLANNED A FAMILY TRIP to Costa Rica the summer before she went off to college. But my husband couldn't get away from work, so my daughter and I ended up spending three days at a beautiful eco-tourist resort. We had a wonderful time together, and it was definitely special because it was just the two of us. It wasn't meant to be this way, but it ended up working out really well. If you can get away to a special place for a few days with your college-bound child, you should do it.

> —LUCY RUMACK
> BROOKLYN, NEW YORK
> 🎓 1
> 🏛 SWARTHMORE COLLEGE

AFTER 18 YEARS, their room at home is empty overnight. At the school drop-off, after you unload the car and drag a few boxes up to the little dorm room, be prepared for your child to head off with her new friends within 10 minutes. You will spend that night alone at dinner or alone waiting for the plane at the airport. Get used to that same feeling if you ever visit again. Keep telling yourself it is all good; it's what is supposed to happen, if you did your job right.

—TOM
SAN FRANCISCO, CALIFORNIA
🎓 1
🏛 UNIVERSITY OF ARIZONA

• • • • • • • •

Before you leave them at school, get a list of phone numbers of their roommates and some of their friends. It made me feel so much better to have those numbers as I drove away.

—CAMILLE
CINCINNATI, OHIO
🎓 1
🏛 UNIVERSITY OF KENTUCKY

I HAVE ONE CHILD, and after 18 years of living with him, it felt like I was losing a limb. Nothing could ease the pain, but to make it a little bit more bearable, I bought us both video cameras so that we could keep in touch while he was away. We speak two to three times a week through our instant messaging program and video. The sound and picture are great, and it's free.

—BERNIE
HOUSTON, TEXAS
1
NORTHWESTERN UNIVERSITY

· · · · · · · · ·

WHEN I DROPPED MY SON OFF AT COLLEGE, it was bitter-sweet. He is attending my alma mater, so when I brought him up to the school it was hard for me to leave. My other son was like, "Get in the car, Mom," because I was taking so long to leave. But, it was more of a sense of pride that I had an African American male that didn't end up being a statistic. It was a wonderful feeling—not of sadness, but a feeling that "my little boy is growing up."

—GLYNIS RAMOS-MITCHELL
ATLANTA, GEORGIA
2
MIDDLEBURY COLLEGE;
UNIVERSITY OF MASSACHUSETTS, AMHERST

USEFUL WEB SITES

Check these sites for whatever information you may need. In addition, the Web sites of each college or university you are interested in will provide specific information.

FUNDING

Ameri-Corps National & Community Service
www.cns.gov

Gates Millennium Scholars
www.gmsp.org

FAFSA Express
www.fafsa.ed.gov

FastWEB
www.fastweb.com

The Financial Aid Information Page
www.finaid.org

Free Scholarship Search
www.freschinfo.com

Sallie Mae Scholarship Service
www.scholarships.salliemae.com

Scholarship Search
apps.collegeboard.com/cbsearch_ss/welcome.jsp

Student Advantage
www.studentadvantage.com/static university_fundraising.shtml

The Student Guide
studentaid.ed.gov

Higher Education Services Organization
www.hesc.com

NCAA Guide for the College Bound Student Athlete
www.ncaa.org

Unusual Scholarships
finaid.org/scholarships/unusual.phtml

Expected Family Contributions Calculator
apps.collegeboard.com/fincalc/efc_welcome.jsp

Financial Aid Calculators
www.finaid.org/calculators/finaidestimate.phtml

Student Loan Finder
www.estudentloan.com

Scholarship Searches
www.collegenet.com
www.scholarship.com

Minority Online Information Service
http://www.molis.org

ORIENTATION

US Department of Education
www.ed.gov/gearup/index.html

Campus Tours
www.campustours.com

The U
www.theu.com

College Bound Network
www.cbnet.com

FINDING YOUR SCHOOL

College Board
www.collegeboard.com

Peterson's Education Center
www.petersons.com

Project EASI (Easy Access for Students and Institutions)
www.asi.ed.gov

RESOURCES FOR SCHOOLS AND FAMILIES

Universal Black Pages
www.ubp.com

US News & World Report
www.usnews.com/sections/education

American Universities
www.clas.ufl.edu/CLAS/american-universities.html

College Opportunities Online
www.nces.ed.gov/ipeds/cool

American Association of Community Colleges
www.aacc.nche.edu

Community College Web
www.mcli.dist.maricopa.edu/cc

Database of Colleges
www.collegenet.com
www.gocollege.com

College Search Sites
www.princetonreview.com
www.campusdirt.com
www.collegeconfidential.com
www.collegeprowler.com

TESTING & APPLYING

The American College Testing Program
www.act.org

Educational Testing Services
www.ets.org

TEST.com
www.test.com

Princeton Review
www.review.com

Sylvan Learning
www.educate.com

The Common Application
www.commonapp.org

College View
www.collegeview.com/applica-tion/index.html

Kaplan On-Line
www.kaplan.com

SAT
www.collegeboard.org/sat

TOEFL
web1.toefl.org

College Link
www.collegelink.com

College Net
www.collegenet.com

Thick Envelope
www.thickenvelope.com

COUNSELING

National Association for College Admission Counseling

www.nacacnet.org

College Horizons
www.whitneylaughlin.com

Internet Guide for Parents
www.guideforparents.com

GAP YEAR PROGRAMS

www.gap-year.com
www.yearoutgroup.org
www.leapnow.org/home.htm
www.bunac.org
www.interimprograms.com
www.transitionsabroad.com
www.traveltree.co.uk

MISCELLANEOUS

College Is Possible
www.collegeispossible.org

Council for Opportunity in Education
www.coenet.us

Initiative on Educational Excellence for Hispanic Americans
www.yesican.gov

The Chronicle of Higher Education
http://chronicle.com

SPECIAL THANKS

Thanks to our intrepid "headhunters" for going out to find so many respondents from around the country with interesting advice to share:

Jamie Allen, Chief Headhunter

Andrea Parker	Lorraine Calvacca
Andrea Syrtash	Nancy Larson
Brandi Fowler	Paula Andruss
Daniel Nemet-Nejat	Ruthann Spike
Helen Bond	Staci Siegel (Rokas Corp.)

Thanks, too, to our editorial advisor Anne Kostick. And thanks to our assistant, Miri Greidi, for her yeoman's work at keeping us all organized. The real credit for this book, of course, goes to all the people whose experiences and collective wisdom make up this guide. There are too many of you to thank individually, but you know who you are.

CREDITS

Page 23: www.collegeboard.com
Page 32: "A Great Year for Ivy League Colleges, but Not So Good for Applicants to Them," *New York Times*, April 4, 2007; www.collegeboard.com
Page 55: www.collegeboard.com Trends in College Pricing 2006; Trends in Student Aid 2006; Education Pays 2006
Page 199: www.collegeboard.com

Other titles in the HUNDREDS OF HEADS® *series:*

HOW TO SURVIVE YOUR FRESHMAN YEAR

"This book proves that all of us are smarter than one of us."

—JOHN KATZMAN
FOUNDER AND CEO, PRINCETON REVIEW

"Voted in the Top 40 Young Adults Nonfiction books."

—PENNSYLVANIA SCHOOL LIBRARIANS ASSOCIATION

"This cool new book ... helps new college students get a head start on having a great time and making the most of this new and exciting experience."

—COLLEGE OUTLOOK

HOW TO SURVIVE GETTING INTO COLLEGE

Book of the Year Award Winner, 2006

—FOREWORD MAGAZINE

"Everyone should have this book!"

—Today Show anchor Meredith Vieira

"....a fun, fascinating read..."

—About.com

"...chock-full of honest, heartfelt and often funny advice..."

—Chicago Sun-Times

HOW TO GET A's IN COLLEGE

Hundreds of successful college students and graduates share their wisdom, stories, tips, and advice on how to get high grades, choose the right major, manage your time, study smart, stay motivated, avoid stress, find the best teachers and courses, form important relationships, and graduate—happily—at the top of your class.

BE THE CHANGE!

"This is a book that could change your life. Read the stories of people who reached out to help somebody else and discovered they were their own ultimate beneficiary. It's almost magic and it could happen to everyone. Go!"

—JIM LEHRER
EXECUTIVE EDITOR AND ANCHOR, NEWSHOUR WITH JIM LEHRER

"An inspiring look at the profound power of the individual to make a positive difference in the lives of others. *Be the Change!* is more than an eloquent tribute to volunteer service—it increases awareness of our shared humanity."

—ROXANNE SPILLETT
PRESIDENT, BOYS & GIRLS CLUBS OF AMERICA

"Civic involvement is an enriching joy, as the people in this book make clear. It's also what makes America so great. This is a wonderful and inspiring book."

—WALTER ISAACSON
CEO, ASPEN INSTITUTE

ABOUT THE EDITOR

RACHEL KORN is a U.S. college advisor and consultant. She attended Brandeis University as a Justice Brandeis Scholar, and Harvard University, where she earned a Master's Degree in Higher Education Administration. Rachel worked on the admissions staffs at Wellesley College, Brandeis University, and the University of Pennsylvania, where she visited hundreds of high schools across the nation, interviewed prospective students, and read and advised committees on approximately 10,000 applications. She has been an active member of several professional organizations, including regional chapters of the National Association for College Admissions Counseling, the College Board, and NAFSA: Association of International Educators. Rachel also serves as Higher Education and Admissions Consultant for Nirshamim.co.il, Israel's Web portal for U.S. study, supported by the U.S. Embassy. She currently lives in Tel Aviv, Israel.

VISIT WWW.HUNDREDSOFHEADS.COM

Do you have something interesting to say about college, marriage, pregnancy, children, dieting, holding a job, or one of life's other challenges?

- Help humanity—share your story!
- Get published in our next book.
- Find out about the upcoming titles in the HUNDREDS OF HEADS® survival guide series.
- Read up-to-the-minute advice on many of life's challenges.
- Sign up to become an interviewer for one of the next HUNDREDS OF HEADS® survival guides.